A STUDENT'S GUIDE TO U.S. HISTORY

ISI GUIDES TO THE MAJOR DISCIPLINES

GENERAL EDITOR   EDITOR

JEFFREY O. NELSON   WINFIELD J. C. MYERS

A STUDENT'S GUIDE TO PHILOSOPHY
BY RALPH M. MCINERNY

A STUDENT'S GUIDE TO LITERATURE
BY R. V. YOUNG

A STUDENT'S GUIDE TO LIBERAL LEARNING
BY JAMES V. SCHALL, S.J.

A STUDENT'S GUIDE TO THE STUDY OF HISTORY
BY JOHN LUKACS

A STUDENT'S GUIDE TO THE CORE CURRICULUM
BY MARK C. HENRIE

A STUDENT'S GUIDE TO U.S. HISTORY
BY WILFRED M. MCCLAY

A STUDENT'S GUIDE TO ECONOMICS
BY PAUL HEYNE

A STUDENT'S GUIDE TO POLITICAL THEORY
BY HARVEY C. MANSFIELD, JR.

A Student's Guide to U.S. History

WILFRED M. MCCLAY

ISI BOOKS
WILMINGTON, DELAWARE

The Student Self-Reliance Project and the ISI Guides to the Major Disciplines are made possible by grants from the Philip M. McKenna Foundation, the Wilbur Foundation, F. M. Kirby Foundation, Castle Rock Foundation, the William H. Donner Foundation, and other contributors who wish to remain anonymous. The Intercollegiate Studies Institute gratefully acknowledges their support.

Cataloging-in-Publication Data

McClay, Wilfred M.
     A student's guide to U.S. history / by Wilfred M. McClay.
  —1st ed. —Wilmington, DE : ISI Books, 2000.

    p. ; cm.

    ISBN 1-882926-45-5
       1. United States—History—Outlines, syllabi, etc.
    I. Title. II. Title: Guide to U.S. history

E178.2 .M23 2000   00-101236
973—dc21   CIP

Published in the United States by:

    ISI Books
    Post Office Box 4431
    Wilmington, DE 19807-0431

Cover and interior design by Sam Torode
Manufactured in Canada

CONTENTS

WHAT THIS GUIDE IS, AND ISN'T

❧

THE RATIONALE FOR this small book may not be immediately clear. There is already an abundance of practical guide-books for the study of history, some of them very good. There already are, for example, helpful manuals offering direction to those undertaking historical research and writing, books touching upon every conceivable problem, from the selection and use of source materials to questions of prose style, and of proper form for source notes and bibliographical entries. There are short histories offering a highly compressed account of American* history, if that is what is wanted—and such books can be very useful for beginning students and experienced teachers alike. There are bibliographical reference works aplenty, general and specialized, which, when used in tandem with the source notes and bibliographies found in the best secondary works in a given field, can quickly provide a reasonably good sense of that field's scholarly topography. What, then, can one hope to accomplish in this short work that has not already been done better by others?

---

* I will be using the term "America" interchangeably with the term "United States," although fully recognizing that there is a sense in which both Canada and Latin America are "American."

The answer is that this book tries to do something different. It is not meant to be a compendium, let alone a comprehensive resource. It will not substitute for an outline of American history or other brief textbook, and its bibliographical resources are intentionally brief and somewhat idiosyncratic. It does not pretend to offer practical advice as to how to do research. It does not inquire into the state of the discipline, or what methods and theories might currently be on "the cutting edge" (to use one of the dullest metaphors around), let alone what may be coming next. If you are in search of such things you will need to look elsewhere.

Instead, this book attempts to do something that is both smaller and bigger than those aims. It attempts to identify and express the ultimate rationale for the study of American history, and provide the student with a relief map of the field's permanent geography—which is to say, of the largely unchanging issues that have undergirded and enlivened successive generations of historical study. A secure knowledge of that ultimate rationale, the *telos* of historical study, is the most essential piece of equipment required to approach American history intelligently and profitably, precisely because it gives one a vivid sense of what is enduringly at stake.

That sense is all too often missing from history courses and textbooks. Sometimes it is missing because teachers and authors silently presume such knowledge in their audiences. Sometimes, though, it is missing because they have lost sight of it themselves, whether because they are absorbed in the demands of their particular projects, blinkered by a professionalized ethos, or blinded by the preconceptions of ideology. It would be nice to report that this trend shows signs of reversal. But if anything the opposite is the case. So, unless you are blessed with uncommonly thoughtful teachers, as a student of history you will have to dig in and do for yourself the work of integration, of asking what it all means. I hope this book will help.

I have not striven for originality, precisely because it is my hope that this book will not become readily outdated. History, like all fields of study in our day, is highly subject to the winds of fashion. There is no getting around this fact entirely, just as one cannot entirely avoid fashion in clothing. (Even being stodgily unfashionable is a "fashion statement," and the vanity of the man who will never wear anything fashionable in public, out of fear of being thought vain, is vanity just the same.) So I will not pretend to be immune, and I also respectfully decline to play the role of the old fogey, who thinks all innovation in historical scholarship is humbug. Would that it were that easy to distinguish gold from dross. Nevertheless, I try to look beyond the ebb and flow of fashion in this book, and attempt to draw our attention instead to the more permanent questions.

What follows, then, is divided into several sections. I begin with introductory essays about the character and meaning of historical study in general, leading into an examination of the special questions and concerns animating the study of American history. These are followed by a series of short essay-sketches, which I call "windows," offering us brief glimpses of the central and most characteristic themes of American history, with several suggested readings. Following that, I have provided a short and decidedly nonexhaustive list of caveats, warnings about certain practical pitfalls to avoid. Finally, there is a very short "American Canon," the handful of essential books that I believe all students of American history simply *must* read.

HISTORY AS LABORATORY
༄

WHAT IS HISTORY? One answer might be: It is the science of incommensurable things and unrepeatable events. Which is to say that it is no science at all. We had best be clear about that from the outset. This melancholy truth may be a bitter pill to swallow, especially for those zealous modern sensibilities that crave precision more than they covet accuracy. But the fact of the matter is that human affairs, by their very nature, cannot be made to conform to the scientific method—not, that is, unless they are first divested of their humanness. The scientific method is an admirable thing, when used for certain purposes. You can simultaneously drop a corpse and a sack of potatoes off the Tower of Pisa, and together they will illustrate a precise law of science. But such an experiment will not tell you much about the human life that once animated that plummeting body—its consciousness, its achievements, its failures, its progeny, its loves and hates, its petty anxieties and large presentiments, its moments of grace and transcendence. Physics will not tell you who that person was, or about the world within which he lived. All those things will have been edited out, until only mass and acceleration remain.

By such a calculus our bodies may indeed become indistinguishable from sacks of potatoes. But thankfully that is not the calculus of history. You won't get very far into the study of history with such expectations, unless you choose to confine your attention to inherently trivial or boring matters. In which case, studying history will soon become its own punishment. One could propose it as an iron rule of historical inquiry that there is an inverse proportionality between the importance of the question and the precision of the answer. This should not be taken as an invitation to be gassy and grandiose in one's thinking, a lapse that is in its own way just as bad as being trivial. Nor is it meant as an indirect swipe at the use of quantitative methods in history, which are indispensable and which, when properly employed, can lead to insights of the highest order. Nor does it challenge Pascal's mordant observation that human beings are, in some respects, as much automatons as they are humans. It merely asserts that the genuinely interesting historical questions are irreducibly complex, in ways that exactly mirror the irreducible complexity of the human condition. Any author who asserts otherwise should be read skeptically—and, life being short, quickly.

Take, for example, one of the most fascinating of these issues: the question of what constitutes greatness in a leader. The word "great" itself implies a comparative judgment. But how do we go about making such comparisons intelligently? There are no quantitative units into which we can translate, and no scales upon which we can weigh the leadership quotients of Pericles, Julius Caesar, Genghis Khan, Attila, Elizabeth I, Napoleon, Lincoln, and Stalin. We can and do compare such leaders, however—or others like them, such as the long succession of American presidents—and learn extremely valuable things in the process. But in doing so, can we detach these leaders from their contexts, and treat them as pure abstractions? Hardly. Otherwise we could not know whom they were leading, where they were going, and what they were up against. If made entirely without context, comparisons are meaningless. But if made entirely within context, comparisons are impossible.

So there is a certain quixotic absurdity built into the very task historians have taken on. History strives, like all serious human thought, for the clarity of abstraction. We would like to make its insights as pure as geometry, and its phrases as effortless as the song warbled by Yeats's golden bird of Byzantium. But its subject matter—the tangled lives of human beings, in their unique capacity to be both subject and object, cause and effect, active and passive, free and situated—forces us to rule out that goal in advance. Modern historians have sworn off forays into the ultimate. It's just not part of their job description. Instead, their generalizations are always generalizations of the middle range, carefully hedged about by qualifications and caveats.

This can, and does, degenerate into such an obsession with conscientious nuance that modern historians begin to sound like the J. Alfred Prufrocks of the intellectual world—

self-henpecked, timid, and bloodless, never daring to eat a peach unless they are certain that they're doing it in proper context. Yet there is something admirable in their modesty. It is the genius of history to be always aware of limits and boundaries. History reminds us that the form and pressure imparted by our origins linger on in us. It reminds us that we can never entirely remove the incidentals of our time and place, because they are never entirely incidental. Nor can we ever reduce what we know about ourselves to a set of propositions, because what we know about ourselves, or think we know, soon becomes a part of what we are—and at the very moment we absorb those propositions, we inch beyond them. Self-knowledge is hard to come by, even for those rare individuals who actually seek it, because the target is always moving. But writing history well may be harder, because it means taking ever-moving aim at an ever-moving target with ever-changing eyes, ever-transforming weapons, and ever-protean intentions. Exhilarating, yes. But not without its dangers and frustrations.

So perhaps the Greek philosopher Heraclitus, who famously asserted that one could not step into the same river twice, was the first and best theorist of history. But stepping into the same river twice seems almost manageable when compared to the challenge of finding and rightly interpreting the past's precedents and parallels. Such appropriation of the past is a paradoxical, ironic undertaking, because it becomes progressively more difficult precisely as one becomes more skilled, knowledgeable, and conscientious.

It is surprisingly easy to write bad history, and even easier to make crude if profound sounding historical comparisons. It is easy, for example, for any layman to opine portentously that there are ominous parallels between the histories of America and Rome, or between America and the Weimar Republic. And so it may be. But it is very difficult for experienced and knowledgeable historians to specify wherein those parallels are to be found—so hard that, these days, they will almost certainly refuse to try, particularly since they have no professional incentive to do so. It is easy for armchair wits to compare Thomas Jefferson and Bill Clinton, or for pundits to rank the American presidents in serial order, or for journalists to pillage the past for anecdotes and easy generalizations about the electoral fortunes of vice presidents and third parties. But it is maddeningly difficult for those who really know their subject, and understand the ever-present contingency and unpredictability of history, to make such judgments, without becoming all knotted up in qualifiers and exceptions.

It is easy to treat the past as if it were an overflowing, open grab bag, and historians are right to admonish those who do so. But only partly right. Because man does not live by pedantry and careful contextualization alone. If the study of history is important, then there can be no doubt that it is proper—and necessary—for us to seek out precedents in the past, and to do so energetically and earnestly. Those few precedents are the only clues we have about the likely outcomes for similar endeavors in the present and future.

History, then, is a laboratory of sorts. By the standards of science, it makes for a lousy laboratory. No doubt about that.

But the problem is, it is all that we have. It is the only laboratory available to us for assaying the possibilities of our human nature *in a manner consistent with that nature.* Far from disdaining science, we can and should imitate many of the characteristic dispositions of science—the fastidious gathering and sifting of evidence, the effort to be dispassionate and evenhanded, the openness to alternative hypotheses and explanations, the caution in propounding sweeping generalizations. Although we will continue to draw upon history's traditional storytelling structure, we also can use sophisticated analytical models to discover patterns and regularities in individual and collective behavior. We even can call what we are doing "social science" rather than history, if we like.

But we cannot follow the path of science much further than that, if only for one stubborn reason: we cannot devise replicable experiments, and still claim to be studying human beings, rather than corpses. It is as simple as that. You cannot experiment upon human beings, at least not on the scale required to make history "scientific," and at the same time continue to respect their dignity as human beings. To do otherwise is like murdering to dissect. It is not science but history that tells us that this is so. It is not experimental science, but history, that tells us how dreams of a "worker's utopia" gave rise to one of the most corrupt tyrannies of human history, or how civilized, technically competent modern men fashioned the skin of their fellow men into lampshades. These are not experiments that need to be replicated. Instead, they need to be remembered, as pieces of evidence about what civilized men are still capable of doing, and the kinds of political regimes and moral reasonings that seem likely to unleash—or to inhibit—such moral horrors.

Thankfully, not all of history's lessons are so gruesome. The history of the United States, for example, provides one reason to hope for the continuing improvement of the human estate, and such sober hopefulness is, I believe, reinforced by an honest encounter with the dark side of that American past. Hope is not real and enduring unless it is based upon the truth, rather than the power of positive thinking. The dark side is always an important part of the truth, just as everything that is solid casts a shadow when placed in the light. Chief among the things history should teach us, especially those of us who live nestled in the comfortable bosom of a prosperous America, is what Henry James called "the imagination of disaster." The study of history can be sobering and shocking, and morally troubling. One does not have to believe in original sin to do it successfully, but it probably helps. By relentlessly placing on display the pervasive crookedness of humanity's timber, history brings us back to earth, equips us to resist the powerful lure of radical expectations, and reminds us of the grimmer possibilities of human nature—possibilities that, for most people living in most times, have not been the least bit imaginary. With such realizations firmly in hand, we are far better equipped to move forward in the right way.

So we work away in our makeshift laboratory, deducing what we can from the patient examination and comparison of singular examples, each deeply rooted in its singular place and moment. From the perspective of science, this is a crazy way to go about things. It is as if we were reduced to making deductions from the fragmentary journal of a mad scientist who constructed haphazard experiments at random, and never repeated any of them. But that oddness is unavoidable. It indicates how different is the approach to knowledge afforded by the disciplines we call the humanities, among whose number history should be included.

The humanities are notoriously hard to define. But at their core is a determination to understand human things in human terms, without converting or reducing them into something else. Such a determination grounds itself in the phenomenology of the world as we find it, including the thoughts, emotions, imaginings, and memories that have gone to make up our picture of reality. Science tells us that the earth rotates upon its axis while revolving around the sun. But in the domain of the humanities, the sun still also rises and sets, and still establishes in that diurnal rhythm one of the deepest and most universal symbols of all the things that rise and fall, or live and die. There are, in short, different kinds of truth, and we need all of them in order to live.

HISTORY AS MEMORY

ALL THE ABOVE considerations argue, in some sense, for the *usefulness* of history. But the sources of our historical urges are even more primal than that. We do history even when it is not particularly useful, simply because human beings are, by their nature, remembering creatures and storymaking creatures. History is merely the intensifying and systematizing of these basic human attributes. Historical consciousness is to civilized society what memory is to individual identity. Without memory, and the stories within which memories are held suspended, one cannot say who or what one is; one cannot learn, use language, pass on knowledge, raise children, establish rules of conduct, or even dwell in society, let alone engage in science. Nor can one have a sense of the future as a moment in time that we know will come, because we remember that other tomorrows have come too. The philosopher George Santayana had this in mind when he wrote what were perhaps his most famous words, in his *Reason in Common Sense*:

> Progress, far from consisting in change, depends on retentiveness. When change is absolute there remains no being to improve and no direction is set for possible improvement: and when experience is not retained, as among savages, infancy is perpetual. Those who cannot remember the past are condemned to repeat it. In the first stage of life the mind is frivolous and easily distracted, it misses progress by failing in consecutiveness and persistence. This is the condition of children and barbarians, in which instinct has learned nothing from experience.

A culture without memory will necessarily be barbarous, no matter how technologically advanced and sophisticated, because the daily drumbeat of artificial sensations and amplified events will drown out all other sounds, including the strains of an older music.

Speaking of history as memory may seem to clash with our common notions of history as the creation of a definitive "record" or chronicle, a copious account of bygone events which is placed on a prominent shelf and consulted as needed, as if it were a small-scale secular equivalent of the Book of Life. We should be thankful for the existence of such accounts—chronicles of organizations, communities, churches, families—often produced in a remarkably selfless spirit, which form the backbone of the historical enterprise. But of what use is even the most copious historical record if it is never incorporated into human consciousness, never made into an integral part of the world as we see it, never permitted to carry the past's living presence into the present, where it can enliven the inertness of the world as it is given to us? In this sense, antiquarianism sometimes does not serve history well. It is a good thing to keep records, but a very bad thing to do nothing but lock them away in the archives to gather dust. Written history that is never incorporated into human awareness is like written music that is never performed, and thus never heard.

The growing professionalization of historical writing in the past hundred years has only accelerated this very problem, very much contrary to the hopes of the early advocates for professionalization, who had hoped to make history a useful science. For most of today's professional historians, the suggestion that their work might be so written as to address itself to a general public is unthinkable. Instead, the process of professionalization has carved the study of history up into smaller and narrower pieces, more and more manageable but less and less susceptible of meaningful integration or synthesis.

There is not a sinister conspiracy behind this. Our professional historians do not, by and large, go out of their way to be obscure or inaccessible. They are hardworking, conscientious, and intelligent people. But their graduate training, their socialization into the profession of historical writing, and the structure of professional rewards and incentives within which they work, have so completely focused them upon the needs and folkways of their guild that they find it exceedingly hard to imagine looking beyond them. Their sins are more like those of sheep than those of wolves.

Add to this, however, the fact that, for a small but increasing number of our academic historians, the principal point of studying the past is to demonstrate that all our inherited institutions, beliefs, conventions, and normative values are arbitrary—"social constructions" in the service of power—and therefore without legitimacy or authority. For them, history is useful not because it tells us about the things that made us who we are, but because it releases us from the power of those very things, and thereby confers the promise of boundless possibility. All that has been constructed can presumably be dismantled and reconstructed, and all contemporary customs and usages, being *merely* historical, can be cancelled. In this view, it would be absurd to imagine that the past should have anything to teach us, or the study of the past any purpose beyond the needs of the present. History's principal value, in this view, is not as a glue but <u>as a solvent.</u>

We can grant some admixture of truth in these assertions. In the first place, scrupulous history cannot be written to please the crowd. And yes, history ought to be an avenue whereby the present escapes from the tutelary influence of the past. But the study and teaching of history ought to be directed not only at the accumulation of historical knowledge and the overturning of myths and legends, but also at the cultivation of a historical consciousness. This means that history is also an avenue whereby the present can escape, not only from the past, but from the *present*. Historical study ought to enlarge us, deepen us, and draw us out of ourselves, by bringing us into a serious encounter with the strangeness—and the strange familiarity—of a past that is already a part of us. In drawing us out, it "cultures" us, in all the senses of that word. As such, it is not merely an academic subject or a body of knowledge, but a formative discipline of the soul. Historians should not forget that they fulfill an important public purpose simply by doing what they do. They do not need to justify themselves by their contributions to the formulation of public policy. They do their part when they preserve and advance a certain kind of consciousness and memory, traits of character that a culture of relentless change and instant erasure has all but declared war upon. To do that alone is to do a great deal.

Let me touch on one final general consideration, relating

to historical truth. There are two characteristic fallacies that arise when we speak of truth in history—and we should be wary of them both. The first is the confident belief that we can know the past definitively. The second is the resigned conviction that we can never know the past at all. They are, so to speak, the respective fallacies of positivism and skepticism, stripped down to their essences. They are the mirror images of one another. And they are equally wrong.

The first fallacy has lost some of its appeal for academic historians, but not with the public. One hears this particular reliance upon the authority of history expressed all the time, and most frequently in sentences that begin, "History teaches us that…" Professional historians and seasoned students, to their credit, tend to cringe at such words. And indeed, it is surprising, and not a little amusing, to see how ready the general public is to believe that history, unlike politics, is an entirely detached, objective, impersonal, and unproblematic undertaking. Not only the unsophisticated make this error. Even the jaded journalists who cover the White House, and the politicians they cover, imagine that the question of a particular president's historical standing will be decided by the impartial "verdict of history." I say surprising and amusing, but such an attitude is also touching, because it betrays such immense naive confidence in the transparency of historical authority. Many people still believe that, in the end, after all has been done and said, History Speaks.

Whatever their folly in so believing, however, it does not justify a movement to the opposite extreme—the dogmatic skepticism and relativism implicit in the second fallacy. That, in its crudest form, is the belief that all opinions are created equal, and since the truth is unknowable and morality is subjective, we all are entitled to think what we wish, and deserve to have our opinions and values respected, so long as we don't insist too strenuously upon their being "true." Such a perspective is not only wrong, but subtly disingenuous, and damaging to the entire historical undertaking.

It is disingenuous, because if you scratch a relativist or a postmodernist, you invariably find something else underneath—someone who operates with a full panoply of unacknowledged absolutes, such as belief in universal human rights and in the pursuit of the highest degree of personal liberation. Generally, too, there is an assumption that history is a tale of unjust exploitation, oppression, and domination—though just where one derives those pesky concepts of injustice, oppression, et al., which in turn presume concepts of justice and equity, is not stated. Indeed, because those absolutes are never acknowledged as such, they are rendered peculiarly nonnegotiable. The virulence with which they are asserted serves to mask their lack of rational basis.

Hence, we have the curious fact that relativism and social constructionism are applied in a very selective way—always, for example, to the deconstruction of traditional gender roles and what some historians of the family tendentiously label "the cult of domesticity," never to the deconstruction of modern feminist ideology. When the deconstructive technique comes up against such a privileged ideological default setting, it automatically shuts down. No wonder that an era in which postmodernism has had such an impressive run should also be an era dominated by accusations of "political correctness." The logic of postmodernism should mean that it is applied to any and all subjects. The fact that it is so selectively applied is a devastating commentary on the spirit in which it is used. It removes the protections of conventional evidence-gathering from one class of subjects, while keeping those protections, and much more, in place for others. Such a gambit can control discourse and silence opposition, for a time. But it cannot persuade.

Which leads, finally, to the reason why the second fallacy is so damaging. Quite simply, it renders genuine debate and inquiry impossible. Truth is the basis of our common world. If we cannot argue constructively about historical truth and untruth, and cannot thereby open ourselves to the possibility of persuasion, then there is no reason for us even to talk. If we cannot believe in the reasonable fixity of words and texts, then there is no reason for us to write. If we cannot believe that an author has something to offer us beyond the mere fact of his or her "situatedness," then there is no reason for us to read. If we cannot believe that there is more to an author, or a book, than a political or ideological commitment then there is no reason for us to listen. If history ever ceases to be the pursuit of truth, then it will in time become nothing more than self-regarding sentimentalism, which in turn masks the sheer will to power, and the war of all against all.

This description sounds rather dire, but in fact, things are not that bad. Whatever we may be saying about what we do, our actions, as readers and writers of history, betray the fact that we continue to believe these things implicitly and would be lost without them. But we would all be better off if we could acknowledge those beliefs explicitly—and thereby make them available for rational examination. This need not entail the tedium of formulating a Philosophy of History, which is generally an enormous distraction from actually studying history. It may be enough to remember the two fallacies, which I will for convenience' sake dub the Fallacy of Misplaced Precision and the Fallacy of Misplaced Skepticism, as the boundary conditions one wants to avoid. There is a world of difference between saying that there is no truth, and saying that no one is fully in possession of it. Yes, the truth is elusive, and only fleetingly and partially glimpsed outside the mind of God. But it is no folly to believe that the truth *is* there, and that we are drawn by our nature to search endlessly for it. Indeed, the real folly is in claiming otherwise.

RETHINKING AMERICAN HISTORY

PERHAPS YOU ARE surprised that I have preceded my treatment of American history with such lengthy and slightly abstruse philosophical discussions about the nature of history. Isn't American history, when all is said and done, a rather nuts-and-bolts subject? But I did this quite deliberately. All too many of us who grew up and were educated in the United States were taught, albeit not always consciously, to regard American history as rather thin and provincial gruel, a subject appealing only to intellectually limited people, who do not mind forgoing the rich and varied fare of European history. Many a high-school American history course offered by a bored, dry-as-dust pedagogue who doubled as the wrestling or basketball coach has reinforced that impression. Such courses tended to offer American history as a cut-and-dried succession of tiresome clichés and factoids, whose importance was, to an adolescent mind, either unclear or self-evidently nugatory: the terms of the Mayflower Compact, the battles between Hamilton and Jefferson, the provisions of the Missouri Compromise, Jackson's Bank War, the origins of "Tippecanoe and Tyler, Too," the Wilmot Proviso, the meaning of "Rum, Romanism, and Rebellion," the difference between the CWA and the WPA and the CCC and the PWA, and so on, and on. Such stupefying courses of study, endless parades of trivia punctuated by red-white-and-blue floats bearing plaster of Paris busts of inspirational bores, are enough to make one suspect that, when Henry Ford defined history as "one damn thing after another," he must have had American history specifically in mind.

All this is an enormous shame, and profoundly unnecessary. Let me encourage you to sweep away all such narrow preconceptions—and sweep away along with them all narrow filiopietism, and even narrower antifiliopietism, the twin compulsions that so often cripple our thinking about American history—and look at it all afresh. You do not have to decide who you are for and who you are against, who are the heroes and who are the villains. Least of all should you permit the mature study of history to be displaced by Oedipal psychodrama, wherein you symbolically get back at your parents by cheering for the Wobblies and the North Vietnamese (or for the Loyalists and Confederates, as the case may be). Nor, unless you are engaged in a political campaign or ideological crusade—and are therefore not really a serious student of American history—need you choose between the red-white-and-blue and anti-red-white-and-blue renditions of the American past.

Instead, you should think of American history as a drama of incomparable sweep and importance, where all the great questions of human existence and human history—the proper means and ends of liberty, individuality, order, democracy, material prosperity, and technology, among others—have converged, been put into play and brought to a high pitch, and are being worked out and fought over and decided and undecided and revised, even as you read this. It is a drama of enormous consequence, with both praiseworthy and execrable aspects, whose outcome even now is far from certain. There is no need to jazz up American history, or dress it up in colorful period costumes, as if it were a subject that is not inherently riveting. On the contrary. The most consequential themes of human history are here in abundance, every single one of them. Whoever is bored with American history is, to paraphrase Dr. Johnson, bored with life.

Let me quickly add that I am not here falling prey to the unfortunate tendency to make the United States into the cynosure of all human history. Indeed, I would contend that part of the problem is that American history tends to be taught and studied in isolation, when in fact it is a subject that can only be properly understood as part of something much larger than itself—and simultaneously as something much smaller, that insinuates itself into each of our lives. Both these dimensions, the "macro" and "micro" alike, are neglected by our tendency to stick to the flatlands of the middle range. Let us by all means pay our respects to the flatlands. But we should never allow ourselves to be confined to them, lest we lose sight altogether of the inherent sweep and majesty of our subject.

AMERICAN MYTHS AND NARRATIVES

So AMERICAN HISTORY needs to be seen in the context of a larger drama. But there is sharp disagreement over the way we choose to represent that relationship. Is, for example, the nation and culture we call the United States to be understood fundamentally as one built upon the extension of European and especially British laws, institutions, and religious beliefs? Or is it more properly understood as a modern, Enlightenment-based post-ethnic nation built on acceptance of abstract principles, such as universal individual rights, rather than bonds of shared tradition, race, history, conventions, and language? Or is it a transnational and multicultural "nation of nations" in which a diversity of subnational or supernational sources of identity—race, class, gender, ethnicity, national origin, sexual practice, etc.—is the main result sought, and only a thin and minimal sense of national culture and obligation is required? Or is it something else again? And what are the implications of each of those propositions for the answers one gives to the question, "What does it mean for me to be an American?" Clearly each understanding will cause one to answer that question in quite a distinctive way.

All three are weighty and consequential notions of American identity. The one thing they have in common is that they seem to preclude the possibility that the United States is "just another nation." Even nations-of-nations don't grow on trees. Perhaps you will sniff in this statement the telltale residue of American exceptionalism, the debunkers' favorite target. Fair enough. But the fact of the matter is that the very concept of "America" has *always* been heavily freighted with large meanings. It even had a place made ready for it in the European imagination long before Columbus's actual discovery of a Western Hemisphere. From as early as the works of Homer and Hesiod, which located a blessed land beyond the setting sun, to Thomas More's Utopia, to the fervent dreams of English Puritans seeking Zion in the Massachusetts Bay colony, to the Swedish prairie homesteaders and Scotch-Irish hardscrabble farmers and frontiersmen, to the Polish and Italian peasants that made the transatlantic voyage west in search of freedom and material promise, to the Asian and Latin American immigrants that have thronged to American shores and borders in recent decades—the mythic sense of America as an asylum, a land of renewal, regeneration, and fresh possibility, has remained remarkably deep and persistent.

Let us put aside, for the moment, whether the nation has consistently lived up to that persistent promise, whether it has ever been exempted from history, or whether any of the other overblown claims attributed to American exceptionalism are empirically sustainable. Instead, we should concede that it is virtually impossible to talk about America for long without talking about the palpable effects of this mythic dimension. As the sociologists say, whatever is believed to be real, even if it is demonstrably false, is real in its social consequences; and so it does one no good to deny the existence and influence of a mythic impulse that asserts itself everywhere.

It should be well understood, too, that this belief in America's exceptional role as a nation has never in the past been restricted to the political Right. Nor is it so restricted today. Consider the following remarks by former Senator Bill Bradley of New Jersey, in a speech he gave on March 9, 2000, announcing his withdrawal from the race for the Democratic presidential nomination:

> Abraham Lincoln once wrote that "the cause of liberty must not be surrendered at the end of one or even one hundred defeats." We have been defeated. But the cause for which I ran

has not been. The cause of trying to create a new politics in this country, the cause of trying to fulfill our special promise as a nation—that *cannot* be defeated, by one or a hundred defeats.

Senator Bradley was, by all accounts, the more "liberal" of the two Democratic candidates in the 2000 primary season. Yet he found it as comfortable as an old shoe to use this special moment to challenge Americans by speaking the old, old language of "special promise." If that is not a tribute to the persistence of American exceptionalism, then it is hard to imagine what would be.

Almost everyone seems convinced that America, as well as American history, *means* something. To be sure, they don't agree on *what* it means. (Iranian clerics even credit America with being "the Great Satan," a world-historical meaning if there ever was one.) But few permit themselves to doubt *that* American history means something quite distinctive. This impulse has, of course, given recent American historians much of their subject matter; for wherever there are myths, can the jolly debunker be far behind? The myth of the log cabin, the myth of the self-made man, the myth of the virtuous yeoman farmer, the myth of the Virgin Land—the debunking of these myths and others like them has been the stock-in-trade of our American historians. One sometimes wonders what they would be doing with their time were there not such tempting myths to explode.

But one will likely wonder to no purpose, because the chances are exceedingly slim that they will ever find themselves in that predicament. Americans seem disinclined to stop searching for a broad, expansive, mythic way to define their national distinctiveness. They have been remarkably productive at this in the past. Consider the following incomplete list of conceptions, many of which may already be familiar to you, and most of which are still in circulation, in one form or another:

- The City Upon a Hill: America as moral exemplar
- The Empire of Reason: America as the land of the Enlightenment
- Nature's Nation: America as a nation uniquely in harmony with nature
- *Novus Ordo Seclorum:* America as the new order of the ages
- Redeemer Nation: America as redeemer of a corrupted world
- The New Eden: America as land of newness and moral renewal
- The Nation Dedicated to a Proposition: America as land of equality
- The Melting Pot: America as blender and transcender of ethnicities
- Land of Opportunity: America as the nation of material promise and social mobility
- The Nation of Immigrants: America as a magnet for immigrants
- The New Israel: America as God's new chosen nation
- The Nation of Nations: America as a transnational container for diverse national identities

- The First New Nation: America as the first consciously wrought modern nation
- The Indispensable Nation: America as guarantor of world peace, stability, and freedom

In addition to these formulations, there are other, somewhat more diffuse expressions of the national meaning. One of the most pervasive is the idea of America as an *experiment*. This concept of the national destiny was used by none other than George Washington, in his first presidential inaugural address, to denote two things: first, a self-conscious effort to establish a well-ordered, constitutional democratic republic, and second, the contingency and chanciness of it all, the fact that it might, after all, fail if our efforts do not succeed in upholding it. But the idea of the national experiment has, over time, lost its specific grounding in the particulars of the American Founding, and has evolved into something entirely different: an ideal of constant openness to change. "Experimental America" has a tradition, so to speak, but it is a tradition of traditionlessness. In this acceptation, America-as-an-experiment is a pseudoscientific way of saying that none of the premises of our social life are secure: everything is revocable, and everything is up for grabs. One can call this dynamism. One can also call it prodigality.

In any event, none of these mythic constructs enjoys anything like unquestioned predominance in American consciousness. But none is entirely dead either, and some are very much alive. They all work upon, and complicate, the sense of national identity. That there will be more such characterizations devised in years to come seems certain. And that they will give rise to debunking opposition seems just as inevitable. Americans' firm belief that they are distinctive would appear to support a perpetual industry. But my principal point is that such a firm belief is *itself* a datum of great importance, even if debunking historians can prove— Pyrrhic triumph!—that there is not a shred of truth to it. That Americans believe in, and search for the evidence of, their special national destiny is simply a fact of American history. By the twentieth century it had become a fact of world history. The European view of America continued, as it always has, to have a strong element of projection, melding idealization and demonization: America as a vibrant land of innovation, freedom, and possibility, paired with America as an unsettled land of geopolitical arrogance, neurotic restlessness, manic consumerism, and social disorder. For East Asian observers, America the land of individual liberty and dynamism comes in tandem with America the land of intolerable social indiscipline.

That said, however, one has to acknowledge that the sheer number of these mythic versions of America tends to undermine their credibility—just as, when there are too many religions in circulation, all of them begin to look implausible. And so there can be no doubt that, while the desire to discover national meaning continues unabated, the story of American history as told today does not have the same kind of salient and compelling narrative energy that it had fifty or a hundred years ago. Perhaps the myths are too exalted, too inflated, to live by, without egregious hypocrisy or overreaching. In any event, we have, in some measure, lost our guiding national narrative—not completely, but certainly we have lost it as a near-universal article of faith. There is too much self-conscious doubt, too little confidence that the nation-state itself is as worthy of our devotion as is our subgroup. Indeed, the rise of interest in more particularist considerations of race, class, gender, sexuality, ethnicity, religion, and so on have had the effect of draining energy away from the national story, rendering it either weak and indecisive—or the villain in a thousand stories of "subaltern" oppression.

The problem is not that such stories do not deserve to be told. Of course they do. There is always a horrific price to be paid in consolidating a nation, and one is obliged to tell the whole story if one is to count the cost fully. The brutal displacement of Indian tribes, the horrors of chattel slavery and post-emancipatory peonage, the grim conditions of industrial labor, the ongoing tragedy of racial and religious hatred, the hidden injuries of class—all these stories and others like them need to be told and heard, again and again. They should not, however, be told in a way that sentimentalizes them, by displacing the mythic dimension of the American story onto them, and by ignoring the pervasive existence of precisely such horrors and worse in all human societies throughout recorded time. History is not reducible to a simple morality play, and it rarely obliges our moral aspirations in anything but rough form. The crimes, cruelties, inequities, and other misdeeds of American history are real. But they need to be weighed on the scale of *all* human history, if their relative gravity is to be rightly assessed. It is all very well, for example, to be disdainful of corporate capitalism, or postwar suburbia, or any of the other obligatory targets. But the criticism will lack weight and force unless the standard against which corporate capitalism is measured is historically plausible rather than utopian. One can always imagine something better than what is. But the question is, Are there any real historical instances of those alternatives? And what hidden price was paid for *them*? That is the kind of thinking that historians are obliged to engage in.

It is not the content of these more particular stories that constitutes the problem for our dissolving national narrative. It is the fact that the push to tell them, and feature them, has been too successful. The story of American history has been deconstructed into a thousand pieces, a development that has been reinforced and furthered by both professional and ideological motives, but one that is likely in due course to have untoward public effects. Which raises an interesting question: Since throughout history strong and cohesive nations generally have had strong and cohesive historical narratives, how long can we continue to do without one? Do our historians now have an obligation to help us recover one— one, that is, that amounts to something more than a bland-to-menacing general background against which the struggles of smaller groups can be highlighted? Or are the scholarly obligations of historians fundamentally at odds with any public role they might take on, particularly one so prominent? Such a conundrum is not easily resolved. One should, however, at least acknowledge that it exists.

YOUR HISTORY IS AMERICA'S HISTORY—SOMETIMES

ᘄ

ANOTHER COMPELLING REASON to study American history is the simple fact that it is one's own. Obviously, in saying this, I am presuming that my readers will primarily be American students. But the principle involved is universal in character. To understand the history of one's own country, even when one feels oneself to be more or less detached from it, is to gain insight into who one is, and into some of the basic elements of one's makeup. At a minimum, this will result in a rewarding sense of rich historical background that serves to frame and amplify one's own experience—as when one comes to absorb and mentally organize the history of the streets and buildings and neighborhoods of one's city or town. Then even the most routine street scenes reverberate in our consciousness with invisible meanings, intimations that flicker back and forth, again and again, between what we see and what we know.

In the presence of great historical sites, such as the Gettysburg or Antietam battlefields, such awareness takes an even deeper hold of our imaginations and emotions. It is like the sweet melancholy of a solo violin, whose haunting voice pierces us, through all the layers of rationality, with the keen edge of loss. There is a continuity of sorts between such profound emotions and the mingled thoughts and feelings that arise in us when we revisit one of the long-forgotten places of our childhood, or mark the gravestone of someone we have lost. Man is in love, said Yeats, and loves what vanishes. Such is the painful beauty of historical awareness. Our efforts to connect with the vanished past do not necessarily make us happier in any simple sense. But they make us more fully human, and more fully at home in the world, in time as well as space. We fail to honor our full humanity when we neglect them.

Historical study can also unlock the hidden sources of certain ideas, dispositions, and habits in us, by showing us their rootedness in people and events that came before us. In fact, it is not at all far-fetched to understand historical study as bearing a certain resemblance to psychoanalysis in this respect, since both are enterprises intent upon excavating and bringing to conscious awareness the knowledge of consequential antecedents. Indeed, the analogy to individual psychology goes even deeper than that. There comes a point in our personal development when an awareness dawns on us, not only of how profoundly we have been shaped by our own parents and milieu, but just as importantly, of how our parents have been shaped by *their* own parents and milieus, which have in turn been shaped by even earlier sets of parents and milieus, and so on. Once our reflections are set into motion along these lines, our minds crabwalk backward in thought, generation by generation, along the genealogical path, until the path mysteriously peters out and disappears into the mist. This too is a path of historical awareness.

Such an intensely personal approach to history—as a subject telling us about *ourselves*—is more and more popular in our very psychological age. One of the most common ways for high-school and college teachers to get their students interested in history is to ask them to interview their grandparents or (if they have them) great-grandparents, and ask those elders about their own times, and their own experiences and observations. The point is to help students feel personally connected to the abstractions of the past, through people they know—and it works very well. It can serve as a way of giving life to the great story of immigration, or to the rigors of the Great Depression, or to the experiences of the Second World War. Indeed, something of the sort is essential, from time to time, to keep historical study from becoming too bloodless and abstract, too removed from experience. For African Americans and other racial and ethnic minorities, too, it is especially encouraging and stimulating to discover that American history includes *their* lives, and not merely the lives of elite political, business, and military leaders. But they are hardly alone in this need. It is something we all share, and perhaps increasingly so.

To capitalize on this trend, in 1999 the National Endowment for the Humanities announced a millennium project entitled "My History Is America's History." The project's literature enjoins us to "follow your family's story and you will discover America's history." Its website offers links called "Welcome to Our Front Porch"; "Exchange Family Stories," which juxtaposes "your favorite family story" with "America's stories"; "Find Your Place in History," which features a history timeline and history roundtable; and even a link for "Saving Your Family Treasures." What used to be disparaged as mere "genealogy" is now accorded the full status of "history."

As I have said, the general approach is not entirely a bad thing. But this particular way of stating it is troubling. Can it really be true that "my history is America's history"? Or, to put it another way, isn't such an assertion a very, very different matter from saying that "America's history is my history"? The experience of visiting the Gettysburg battlefield that I cited above is an example of the latter emphasis. Such a visit elevates and charges our individual experience by infusing the meaning of the larger into the texture of the smaller— "America" into "me." But what does it mean to go in the other direction—from the droplet to the ocean, as it were— and say that "my family story" is "the American story"? Is this not really a sentimental delusion, a sop to our vanity, and an appeal to our narcissism, on a par with those annoying bumper stickers that boast, "I Can Save the Earth"?

All of which suggests that there are inherent limits to the personalization of history. History can and should be a vehicle for the exploration of self-consciousness. But it also should serve constantly to interrupt the monologues of our self-awareness, and even at times serve as a jamming mechanism. It has to do *both* of these things, and it is not quite doing its job when it fails to do one or the other. The study of history is not only about familiarization but also defamiliarization; not only knowledge of ourselves, but knowledge of that which is *other* than ourselves. That is why we do not study only American history, or only modern history, or only Western history. That, too, is why it is false to say that "my history is America's history," and why the false premise behind such a statement is such a pernicious one. We have to resist the essentially narcissistic idea that history is valueless unless it reflects our own image back to us. One of the uses of the truly usable past lies in its intransigence and otherness, its resistance to us, its unwillingness to oblige our narcissism. Instead history, like all the liberal arts, ought to do what Plato saw as the goal of all inquiry: usher us out of the mental caverns into which we are born, and into the light of a real public world.

A GALLERY OF WINDOWS

NOW COMES THE PLACE in our exposition where we take a slightly more focused and systematic look at some of the characteristic themes of American history. These are, so to speak, the prime numbers of the field, for they cannot easily be factored down into something more basic—although, to be sure, you will see how readily they link, meld, or overlap. They are also the subjects that one finds weaving in and out of virtually every account, every monograph, and every dissertation and term paper written about the American past. They are the perennial problems of American history. For that reason, as you will see, they often are best expressed not as propositional statements but as questions. For that reason, I have chosen to call them "windows" onto the American past, rather than "sketches" or " portraits" of elements in that past, for they function more as frameworks, orienting our line of vision and directing our inquiry, than they do as endpoints or findings for the inquiry itself.

The observer who looks at American history through these windows will not see everything. They are, after all, only windows. I am painfully aware of how much is missing, and had I included every window I would have liked, it would have turned a short book into a tome. Still, I trust that the present text does not miss much of the essential drama. In addition to a brief account of each topic, I will offer several suggestions for further reading. Let me stress that the reading suggestions are made idiosyncratically, without trying to be comprehensive or to showcase what is most recent, and that these suggestions are made over and above the canon readings with which the book concludes.

AMERICA AND EUROPE

We have already gotten a glimpse through this window, in recalling the intensity behind European anticipations of a New World as a place of transformation and renewal. But the tensions created by those anticipations persisted, and became an integral part of American identity: the tension of youth versus age, newness versus heritage, innocence versus experience, naturalness versus artificiality, purity versus corrup-

tion, guilelessness versus sophistication, rawness versus cultivation. America has never been sure how it is related to
Europe, or whether or not it wants to be. From 1776 on,
America has been forever declaring independence from Europe. One sees it in Emerson's famous exhortation, at the end
of his "American Scholar" address of 1837—the speech that
Oliver Wendell Holmes called a "cultural declaration of
independence"—that "we have listened too long to the
courtly muses of Europe," and it is time to find our own
democratic voice.

At the beginning of the twentieth century, American intellectuals renewed the assault, complaining that the blos-
soming of an indigenous American culture was being stifled
by the imposition of an artificial European "genteel tradition," and that it was time for America to "come of age." But
those same intellectuals swooned over the European mod-
ernism of the celebrated Armory Show of 1913, and then
hopped across the ocean to live the expatriate life, and com-
plain, with Ernest Hemingway, about the "broad lawns and
narrow minds" of their native land. The rise of fascism and
Nazism, and Vichy collaborationism, momentarily took a bit
of the luster off of European cultural superiority. But then in
the years after World War II, even as their nation was leading
the Western democracies, America's intellectuals were again
swooning away, this time to the prophetic utterances of European existentialist sages, and more recently, the recondite
texts peddled by the high priests of French poststructuralism.

Such repeated declarations and swoonings lead one to

suspect that the desired independence has never quite occurred. Indeed, it is hard to escape the impression that a nagging American sense of cultural inferiority can be traced in an unbroken line from William Byrd II to George Steiner. Since the Second World War, however, with the ascendancy of the United States to the unquestioned political and military leadership of the West, there has been a partial reversal. This has meant that the relationship has taken on new complexity, in which hostile European intellectuals increasingly identify American culture with all that they find most pernicious in the contemporary world—globalism, mass culture, consumerism, free markets, cultural imperialism, McDonald's hamburgers, and (paradoxically) a persistent weakness for "fundamentalist" religion. Where all this will lead is anyone's guess. But suffice it to say that the mutual obsession of America and Europe is alive and well.

For additional reading, one has to begin with the great novels and novellas of Henry James, whose depiction of the America/Europe dialectic is unsurpassed, especially in *The Wings of the Dove* (N.Y., 1902; London, 1998), *The Ambassadors* (N.Y., 1903; London, 1999), or *The Golden Bowl* (N.Y., 1904; reprinted 1999). For the more recent version of that dialectic, see James W. Ceaser, *Reconstructing America: The Symbol of America in Modern Thought* (New Haven, Conn., 1997). Also useful are C. Vann Woodward, *The Old World's New World* (N.Y., 1991), and Richard Pells, *Not Like Us: How Europeans Have Loved, Hated, and Transformed American Culture Since World War II* (N.Y., 1997).

CAPITALISM

It would be a gross oversight for any primer of American history to neglect the history of American business and economic development. One does not have to be a materialist, Marxian or otherwise, to acknowledge that the nation's remarkable engine of commerce and productivity both exemplified and underwrites much of what is estimable—and some of what is not so estimable—in our past and present. Unfortunately, the standard survey course in American history is likely either to pass over the subject in silence, as one too complex for meat-headed undergraduates, or to treat it as a one-sided morality tale of unending horror, driven by an economic system whose stark inhumanity is so plain that its costs and benefits need not even be measured against any real-world competitors. Many an undergraduate emerging from his professors' lectures on American capitalism can say what Calvin Coolidge said upon being asked about a clergyman's disquisition on sin: "He said he was against it."

Part of the problem is with the word "capitalism." We cannot avoid using it, if for no other reason than that so much of the world associates it so heavily with the United States. But few words are used with more maddening imprecision. By virtue of its being paired so often with "socialism" or "communism," one could easily be led to think that "capitalism" denotes a coherent, systematic theory of economic organization, developed first as a comprehensive abstract philosophy before being tested as a practice. But what we call "capitalism" is actually something very different; it is, for the most part, a set of practices and institutions that were already well established before they became incorporated into an "ism." When we compare capitalism with socialism, we too often are comparing apples and oranges.

In addition, one never knows what the dispraise of "capitalism" is really dispraising. Does it refer to the huge fortunes of industrial tycoons? Or merely to a strong defense of the sanctity of private property? Or a system of structural inequality in the distribution of wealth? Or the ideology of the unregulated free market? Or a cultural habit of acquisitiveness and consumerism? Or a cultural system in which all things are regarded as "commodities," objects for sale? Or a "preferential option" favoring the most unrestricted possible approach to the full range of economic development?

All of these, and more, may be meant at any given time. But one perhaps comes closest to the core of the matter if one sees capitalism as a social system which is so organized as to recognize, protect, and draw upon a unique form of accumulated wealth called "capital." In that sense, the capitalist system is characterized not only by markets, joint-stock companies, private banks, and other instruments of business enterprise and commerce, but by a whole range of institutions made possible by the living and self-perpetuating qualities of accumulated wealth. Among such institutions are the large philanthropic foundations and institutions of higher education which live almost entirely off of their "endowments," which is to say, the "unearned" wealth generated by the unique properties of the capital they possess—capital that generally is accumulated by the Gettys, Vanderbilts, Rockefellers, and Carnegies of the nation's history. One could, with considerable justification, say that there is no more "capitalist" institution than the modern American Ivy League university.

The student who misses out on the history of business (and its natural companion, the history of labor) also misses out on the most far-reaching questions of social organization to be found in the American past. How and why did the republican values of the Founding generation give way to the entrepreneurial liberal capitalism of the nineteenth century, and then to the corporate capitalism of the twentieth? How did the implementation of an industrial system of production, in tandem with the establishment of national networks of distribution, change the character of American society, the structure of organizational life, and the texture of work itself? What are the pluses and minuses entailed in each of these changes? And, looking ahead to the future, is the dynamic of "creative destruction" that many analysts see as the driving force of modern capitalism compatible with a settled and civilized social order? If not, then what can the past tell us about how that force might be effectively tamed or channeled? Or is "creative destruction" a simplistic and unhelpful way to think about the force behind a system as dependent upon a vast array of political, social, legal, cultural, and moral props as capitalism is?

Each of these questions involves fundamental questions of social philosophy, every bit as much as they involve questions of economic organization—for values are implicit in even the most mundane economic decision. After all, even when one is merely "maximizing utility," as the economists like to put it, the meaning of "utility" is far from self-evident. The man who works like a dog to make the money to acquire the Lexus to impress his neighbors is doing something much more complicated than "maximizing utility," something that many of us—including, perhaps, the man himself in a fleetingly lucid moment—would not regard as useful at all.

For additional reading: The dean of historians of American business is Alfred D. Chandler, Jr., and his masterwork, *The Visible Hand: The Managerial Revolution in American Business* (Cambridge, Mass., 1977; reprinted 1980), is must reading, despite its difficulty and its strange de-emphasis on political history. See also Friedrich von Hayek, *Capitalism and the Historians* (Chicago, 1954; reprinted 1963); Drew R. McCoy, *The Elusive Republic: Political Economy in Jeffersonian America* (Chapel Hill, 1980; reprinted 1996); Robert Higgs's splendid *Crisis and Leviathan: Critical Episodes in the Growth of American Government* (N.Y., 1987; reprinted 1989); Joyce Appleby, *Capitalism and a New Social Order: The Republican Vision of the 1790s* (N.Y., 1984); and, as a corrective to the overdrawn portrait of "Robber Barons" in the "Gilded Age"— two long-in-the-tooth epithets that are overdue for retirement—see Burton Folsom, Jr., *The Myth of the Robber Barons: A New Look at the Rise of Big Business in America* (Herndon, Va., 1991; third edition, 1993), and Maury Klein, *The Life and Legend of Jay Gould* (Baltimore, 1986; reprinted 1997). Students who want to see the classic overdrawn portrait in all its gargoyle glory should consult Matthew Josephson, *The Robber Barons: The Great American Capitalists, 1861-1901* (N.Y., 1934; reprinted 1962).

THE CITY

America, asserted historian Richard Hofstadter, was born in the country and has moved to the city. Whether that is true or not, it certainly is true that many Americans have regarded urban life with ambivalence, at best, and as something other than the natural condition of humankind. Thomas Jefferson's fervent belief in the virtuousness of the agricultural life has echoed throughout American history; so too, has the perfervid vision of all great cities as Babylonian fleshpots, brothels, and sinkholes of iniquity, rather than jewels of civilization and refinement. The flight from the city into the suburbs is not a post-World War II innovation; it was already well underway at the end of the nineteenth century, for those few who could afford it. Our contemporary concerns about suburban sprawl and clogged highways need to be seen against this historical background of a strong and persistent American aversion to the urban idea, and a willingness to pay almost any price for even the most fleeting and self-defeating whiff of country life.

But that aversion has to be weighed against an intense fascination with the modern city—its glamour, its industry, its human contrasts, its amazing technological feats, its rich cultural life, its peculiar solitudes, and above all its phenomenal concentration of human energy and dynamism, all memorably captured in the lush pageantry of Walt Whitman's urban poetry. Hofstadter's quip may have accurately described one of the longtime limitations of American historical writing, which took an astoundingly long time to recognize the city as a worthy topic of investigation. But it can hardly be said to describe the attitudes of all Americans. Even more powerful than Jefferson's belief in the moral purity of yeoman farmers has been the belief in the great city as the place of escape, and the avenue of advancement and self-realization, for those fleeing from the confinements and stunted possibilities of rural and small-town life. Even more admirable than Jefferson's design for the University of Virginia's "academical village" was the inspired public vision of Frederick Law Olmsted, who made New York City's Central Park into one of the great urban parks of the world. And infinitely more impressive than the elegant eclecticism of Jefferson's Monticello was the astounding tapering design of Manhattan's Empire State Building, a colossus raised up defiantly, against all odds, during the worst depths of the Great Depression, as a beacon of hope and a monument to American ambition. If there is an abiding American yearning to flee the rootless city for the rooted land, there also is an equal and opposite yearning, whose finest aspect is captured in the stirring, breathcatching sight of that one solitary building, rising with magnificent improbability above the lowlands of Thirty-fourth Street.

For additional reading, see Morton and Lucia White, *The Intellectual Versus the City: From Thomas Jefferson to Frank Lloyd Wright* (Cambridge, Mass., 1962; Westport, Conn., 1981), Jane Jacobs, *The Death and Life of Great American Cities* (N.Y., 1961;

London, 2000), Thomas Bender, *Toward an Urban Vision: Ideas and Institutions in Nineteenth-Century America* (Lexington, Ky., 1975; Baltimore, 1982), and Kenneth Jackson, *Crabgrass Frontier: The Suburbanization of the United States* (N.Y., 1985; reprinted 1987).

EQUALITY

This is one of the keywords of American history, an incantatory concept that commands almost universal assent in contemporary American life. Such inequality as exists in contemporary American society—and of course, there is an enormous amount of it—is tolerated in fact, but it is generally not regarded as justifiable in principle. Belief in equality is a closely held article of faith, against which one dissents at one's peril. The absolute quality of this article of faith of course makes it difficult to explain the hierarchies and asymmetries that in fact exist, and always have existed, and will continue to exist, in American life. Indeed, one of the forces propelling the egalitarian policies of modern American liberalism is the troubled conscience of the privileged, who cannot justify (but will not relinquish) their privileged status within a regime of official equality. Yet it also is true that a culture that does not recognize *any* traditional or ascriptive sources of social and economic rank, or religious justifications for the existing social order, is forced to the conclusion that all such rankings are arbitrary, and therefore unjust. It would appear that there is a dissonance between the way we talk and the way we live.

The historian can impart some valuable ballast to this

discussion by reminding us it was not always thus in American life. The Puritans of Massachusetts Bay, the signers of the Declaration and Framers of the Constitution, the political and cultural leaders of the early national period, North and South—all were comfortable with a considerable measure of hierarchy, and few believed in anything approaching a late-twentieth-century standard of equality, which they would have seen as incompatible with their understanding of liberty. Our era tends to deny the intrinsic tension between equality and liberty, like a man who is simultaneously in love with two women. Such divided attention makes it difficult to do justice to either one, by blinding the ardent lover to the fact that his two amours are rivals.

It is also possible that the current understanding of equality would benefit from the restoration of distinctions that the Founders and Framers would have made, and that Abraham Lincoln would have made, but that have become increasingly unavailable in our own discourse. If "equality" is taken as a global term, meant to encompass social, economic, cultural, and all other forms of equality, then it eventually becomes entirely incompatible with individual liberty. If, however, equality is more narrowly defined as *civic* equality, the political and legal equality of *citizens* in their strictly *public* personae, then it is not only compatible but complementary.

There are, of course, reasonable objections to such a narrow definition of equality, since it fails to take account of crippling disadvantages arising from anterior conditions. To use the most compelling historical example, a strict standard of civic equality would have done almost nothing to help the freedmen emancipated from slavery at the conclusion of the Civil War, since they entirely lacked the economic resources needed for meaningful political freedom, and the means to procure them. One might respond in two ways, however: first, that the abolition of slavery was a special case that should have entailed special obligations (although tragically, those obligations were never acknowledged or met); and second, that the effort to tweak and handicap social results has no logical limits, and therefore is likely to swallow up all social relations, and become the arbitrary patronage tool of whatever party or faction holds political power—unless one limits it from the outset.

As the above indicates, it is impossible to talk for very long about equality (or liberty) in American history without also having to address the institution of slavery. To be sure, one should be careful not to engage in casual generalizations about slavery, since it was an institution of enormous diversity, whose characteristics varied dramatically from region to region, and time period to time period. Even in the relatively short span of American history, there was a wide spectrum of working and living conditions going under that name, ranging from the massive workforce of a Louisiana sugar plantation to the single slave attached to a family farm in Kentucky, and varying dramatically over time in the extent of its openness or repressiveness. But there are certain questions that inevitably arise out of a consideration of slavery—questions that, perhaps more than any others, require of us an extraordinarily mature exercise of the historical imagination. Just how did our slaveholding forebears understand and justify what they were doing? How could so many otherwise morally admirable people fail to see slavery as a crime against humanity—and an egregious violation of fundamental American principles? And how, in answering these questions, can we give the players of the past their full due—the slaveholders as well as the slaves—without surrendering our own moral convictions?

In any event, the theme of equality is of central importance, both to the subject matter of American history and in the minds of the historians who write that history. One cannot fail to be constantly aware of its presence, in studying both the American past and present.

For additional reading, one should begin with the single most illuminating discussion of modern equality, and a "canonical" reading: Alexis de Tocqueville's masterpiece, *Democracy in America* (London, 1835-40; N.Y., 2000). Also useful and illuminating are Robert W. Fogel, *The Fourth Great Awakening and the Future of Egalitarianism* (Chicago, 2000); J. R. Pole, *The Pursuit of Equality in American History* (Berkeley, 1978; revised ed., 1993); and John E. Coons and Patrick M. Brennan, *By Nature Equal: The Anatomy of a Western Insight* (Princeton, N.J., 1999). To get a sense of the variety of slavery, see Ira Berlin, *Many Thousands Gone: The First Two Centuries of Slavery in North America* (Cambridge, Mass., 1998), of its inner life, Eugene D. Genovese, *Roll, Jordan, Roll: The World the Slaves Made* (N.Y., 1974; reprinted 1976), and of its moral contradictions, Edmund Morgan, *American Slavery, American Freedom: The Ordeal of Colonial Virginia* (N.Y., 1975; revised edition, 1995), and Harry V. Jaffa's *Crisis of the House Divided: An Interpretation of the Issues in the Lincoln-Douglas Debates* (N.Y., 1959; revised edition, 1999).

FOUNDING

The United States is distinctive in even having a founding, a clear moment in time in which the nation-state and its institutions were created, in full view of the world, out in the open air. Americans can look to a real Washington and Madison, rather than a legendary Romulus and Remus, as their forebears. Historians, of course, differ about the meaning of the nation's beginnings. Was the establishment of the nation's new constitutional regime really such a dramatic and architectonic moment as the term "founding" implies? Or was it merely a codification into basic law of the shape of an American nation that already existed, and had already been formed decisively by the living legacy of centuries of English law and institutions? Was it truly a founding, in the sense that the principles guiding the Founders and Framers are in some way foundational, permanently necessary for the rest of us, just as the superstructure of a building depends upon its solid foundation? Or was it merely a beginning, the most felicitous deal that could be struck at a given time, opening the way for even more felicitous deals in the years to come? Did it assert a modern idea of politics based upon interest rather than virtue? Or was its modernity tempered and moderated by its simultaneous rootedness in the entire moral and political heritage of the West? And what role did religious conviction and belief in the providential role of America play in the Founding? All of these questions, while a source of endless academic debate, are of far more than academic importance.

For additional reading, one should consult the books cited under "Nation and Federation" below, and James W. Ceaser's work, cited under "America and Europe." In addition, see Forrest McDonald, *Novus Ordo Seclorum: The Intellectual Origins of the Constitution* (Lawrence, Kan., 1985), Russell Kirk, *The Roots of American Order* (Malibu, Cal., 1974; Washington, D.C., 1991), Gordon Wood, *The Creation of the American Republic, 1776-1787* (Chapel Hill, N.C., 1969; reprinted 1998), and Gary L. Gregg, II, ed., *Vital Remnants: America's Founding and the Western Tradition* (Wilmington, Del., 1999).

FRONTIER

Interestingly, in European parlance, a frontier refers to an inviolable boundary or a no-man's-land, often a forbidding and inhospitable place, the edge of something dark and threatening. For Americans, however, the word has a vibrant, almost mystical ring, as the trackless and unsettled territory where civilization renews itself in the quest of exploration by encounter with the unknown and by drinking from the pure springs of unconquered nature. That concept of frontier ran through the literature of the nineteenth century, but found its classic expression in the 1893 lecture of historian Frederick

Jackson Turner, who would immortalize the idea that it was its frontier, not its European heritage, that enabled America to produce a social and political democracy. Turner's thesis has been disproved and disparaged in a hundred ways, but its mythic quality lives on. Small wonder that President John F. Kennedy called his 1960 campaign platform "the New Frontier," and referred to the exploration of space as "the last frontier." Don't expect this kind of talk to end anytime soon.

For additional reading, in addition to Turner's lecture—"The Significance of the Frontier in American History"—see Ray Allen Billington, *Frederick Jackson Turner: Historian, Scholar, Teacher* (N.Y., 1973), and also *Land of Savagery, Land of Promise: The European Image of the American Frontier in the Nineteenth Century* (N.Y., 1980; London, 1985); and Howard R. Lamar, *The Far Southwest, 1846-1912: A Territorial History* (New Haven, Conn., 1966). For a witty debunking of Western myths, see Patricia Nelson Limerick, *The Legacy of Conquest: The Unbroken Past of the American West* (N.Y., 1987).

IMMIGRATION

This is one of the greatest American themes, not only because the United States is largely a nation of immigrants, but because immigration is such a rich metaphor for the kind of personal transformation that America promises—or compels. It captures both what is wonderful and what is heartbreaking about the American experience. Wonderful, in that it symbolizes America's generosity and openness and promise, as the land of a second chance, where the heavy lumber of the Old World could be put aside. Heartbreaking, in that the price paid for pursuing such aspirations was often so high, not only in the broken and blasted lives of those who failed, but in the poignant loneliness of those who succeeded, only to see their children and grandchildren grow into full-fledged citizens of an alien country, with little or no inkling of a former life.

The question of immigration stirs the profoundest sentiments. It is hard for some Americans to accept the cultural diversity and the constant cultural upheaval that come with immigration. They fear that unless immigration is carefully controlled, the basic character of the nation may be altered beyond recognition and thereby undermined. For others, it is hard to imagine their country *without* a steady flow of immigrants and the cultural variety it brings. It has ever been thus. The current controversies over rates of immigration and their effects upon the composition of the nation are nothing new; the subject has always been controversial. Such debates do, however, have their significance, since they go to the heart of the open question of whether America is fundamentally a British or a European or a universalistic or a multicultural nation.

What is sometimes lost in the abstract character of these debates, however, and their tendency to focus on aggregate numbers and inchoate abstractions like "diversity," is a simpler meaning of immigration. Emma Lazarus's 1883 poem "The New Colossus," which appears on a bronze plaque at the base of the Statue of Liberty, is perhaps the best expression of it. Just as Emerson's American Scholar disdained the "courtly muses of Europe," so Lazarus's "mighty woman" refused to emulate the "storied pomp" of the conquering Colossus of Rhodes, preferring a humbler name: "Mother of Exiles." Her joy would not be in luring the powerful and well born, but in embracing the huddled masses and wretched refuse of the earth. To the proud spirit of the Old World she implored: "Send these, the homeless, tempest-tossed, to me." To generations upon generations of the homeless and tempest-tossed—Irish potato farmers, German political refugees, persecuted Russian Jews, Italians, Poles, Greeks, Czechs, Mexicans, Salvadorans, Vietnamese, Cubans, Cambodians, Kosovars—these have not been empty words.

Emma Lazarus came from a sophisticated and refined New York Jewish family. But the sentiments in her poem could have come straight from the biblical prophets and the Christian New Testament—the last shall be first, and the first shall be last; and the stone that was rejected shall become the cornerstone. Such sentiments are an integral part of the warp and woof of American moral life, with its disdain for hereditary privilege, its fondness for underdogs, and its penchant for the second chance. In thinking about immigration, then, we touch upon a subject that engages some of the deepest and most enduring sources of our national soul.

For additional reading, see Oscar Handlin's classic work, *The Uprooted: The Epic Story of the Great Migration that Made the American People* (N.Y., 1951; Boston, 1990), which depicts the immigrant experience as the quintessential experience of modernity; and the aptly titled challenge to Handlin's thesis, John Bodnar's *The Transplanted: A History of Immigrants in Urban America* (Bloomington, Ind., 1985; reprinted 1987), which is a good introduction to the kind of sophisticated scholarship that immigration history has attracted in recent years. Not to be missed is David Hackett Fischer, *Albion's Seed: Four British Folkways in America* (N.Y., 1989).

LIBERTY

With equality, liberty is the other of the two principal pillars in American political ideology. And yet, as Abraham Lincoln pointed out, "The world has never had a good definition of the word liberty. And the American People just now are much in want of one. We all declare for liberty; but in using the same word we do not mean the same thing." This is even more true today then it was in 1864. There is an assumption among modern Americans that their forebears understood liberty in the same freewheeling way modern Americans do. But this is clearly not the case. Interestingly, too, recent writers seem to prefer the slightly more inclusive English term "freedom" over the Latin "liberty," as witness the titles of the two most influential recent large-scale studies of the subject, by historian Eric Foner and sociologist Orlando Patterson. One doesn't want to make too much of this, and indeed, the two words are broadly synonymous in most usage. Generally, however, the noun "liberty" has come to have a mildly archaic ring, and when we use it, we tend to be speaking of a form of *political* freedom, whose existence is predicated upon an entire system of structures and constraints, without whose presence "liberty" is said to devolve into "license." The "freedom" of modern liberalism and libertarianism, which presumes the moral autonomy of the self-validating individual, could not have been further from the Founders' thinking. When Patrick Henry declared, "Give me liberty or give me death," he was not holding out for the expressive liberties of Robert Mapplethorpe.

It may be useful then, though admittedly idiosyncratic—and it is always dangerous to be idiosyncratic with language—to distinguish a "liberty" that enables the individual to act freely within a larger context of moral accountability from a "freedom" that is merely the absence of coercion. One might go even further and add that a "liberty" which has the effect of incorporating citizens more fully and justly in the civil order is very different from a "freedom" that simply keeps government off their backs. Doesn't the former view of liberty, however, assume that we can identify a moral order that is not merely subjective and arbitrary? And in lieu of such a generally acknowledged transpersonal moral order, what are the implications for modern liberty and democracy? Given our obsessive use of the terms "liberty" and "freedom," Americans would do well to reflect on these matters more than we do. There is no need more obvious—and more difficult to achieve—than saying what those two words truly mean, for us as individuals and as a nation.

All this said, however, it is important to stress that for most Americans, and for many people around the world, what makes American liberty so attractive is its friendliness to individual ambition and achievement. The Declaration of Independence speaks not only of the equality of men, but of the "pursuit of happiness" as an inalienable human right; and no modern nation has done more than the United States to enshrine that pursuit. To be sure, we are all too aware of the dismal effects of such pursuit in an era of mass-cultural mendacity and mindless hedonism. But those untoward effects should not blind us to liberty's very considerable virtues. Modern America has become a mecca for the most talented and enterprising people in the world, entrepreneurs, athletes, computer wizards, inventors, and the like, men and women who have come to the United States because they find in it an absence of barriers, and an abundance of incentives, to high achievement. A culture of liberty, properly understood, is a culture devoted to human excellence—not an anti-culture of amoral and anarchic individualism.

Immigrants often grasp such things far better than the native-born, which is one reason why immigration so often serves to renew our sense of America's promise. But they are hardly alone in this. It is not for nothing that the slogan "Be all that you can be!" has been the U.S. Army's single most effective recruiting slogan in the volunteer-army era. For such words, although an admittedly strange way of recruiting young people to a career of national service, nevertheless captured their imaginations, by tapping into their innate longing for a context in which they can test their limits, and have a shot at seeing their capabilities unfold fully. A "liberal" society should do the same thing for all its members.

Yes, there is inequality in America. Some of it is structural, and regrettable. Some of it is perhaps remediable, and we should do whatever we can to provide remedies that do no additional harm. One can argue that any inequality is, in a sense, a barrier to the exercise of liberty. But it is well to remember, too, that there will always be inequality whenever there is a generous measure of genuine liberty—which is to say, so long as the talented and industrious are allowed to work, to strive, to excel, and then to reap the material rewards of their excellence. The alternative to a culture that respects such liberty is a petty, censorious culture, forever wallowing in mediocrity and inefficiency, and mired in forms of poisonous envy that disguise themselves as altruism or "cultural criticism." It is one of liberty's many blessings that it rescues us from such a fate. Long may it prosper.

For additional reading, see Isaiah Berlin, *Four Essays on Liberty* (London, 1969; Oxford, 1982), Orlando Patterson, *Freedom: Freedom in the Making of Western Culture* (N.Y., 1992); and *Freedom: Freedom in the Modern World* (N.Y., 2000), Eric Foner, *The Story of American Freedom* (N.Y., 1998; reprinted 1999), Richard King, *Civil Rights and the Idea of Freedom* (N.Y., 1992; Athens, Ga., 1996), and Michael G. Kammen, *Spheres of Liberty: Changing Perceptions of Liberty in American Culture* (Madison, Wis., 1986; Ithaca, N.Y., 1989). As in most recent academic accounts of liberty, the above works tend to presume the need for heavy state involvement in the securing of liberty, an understanding that is markedly different from what it meant to be "liberal" in the eighteenth and nineteenth centuries. For a more bracing libertarian understanding of these matters, albeit with their own excesses and blind spots, see Virginia Postrel, *The Future and Its Enemies: The Growing Conflict over Creativity, Enterprise, and Progress* (N.Y., 1998); and Jim Powell, *The Triumph of Liberty: A 2,000 Year History Told through the Lives of Freedom's Greatest Champions* (N.Y., 2000).

NATION AND FEDERATION

James Madison said the entity that the Constitution created was a "composition" of national and federal elements. "Federal" in this context, of course, means the opposite of its customary usage; it designates a form of government in which power is constitutionally divided between and among many different levels of government: national government, states, counties, and cities. What made the American brand of federalism something entirely new, very different from the federal idea as it existed in premodern Europe, was the fact that the American national government was meant to have some direct dealings with individual citizens, in addition to its dealings with the respective state governments.

It was a complicated system, itself the fruit of political compromise, and was bound to have constant strains and internal tensions. (In this connection, it is worth thinking for a moment about what an odd name the "United States of America" was in its time, and perhaps still is today.) The Civil War itself was, to a considerable extent, the fruit of those strains and tensions. But the system also has a powerful logic to it, as an intelligent and workable way of dividing political responsibility and authority between and among levels and kinds of government, one that is far more flexible and compelling than we have given it credit for. Moreover, it is an idea whose potential applications suddenly seem far more numerous and fertile. In a world careening at one and the same time toward global economic integration, as well as toward a recrudescent tribalism and national disaggregation, the federative idea behind the U.S. Constitution looks better and better, and top-down centralization and the other alternatives less and less workable.

The federative logic extends back to the imperial system of which the British North American colonies had been a part. Indeed, it makes perfect sense to speak in the same breath of the tensions of the imperial system, the American Revolution, the crisis of the Articles of Confederation, the adoption of the Constitution, the nullification controversy, and the entire series of events leading, as in a Greek tragedy, to the Civil War itself—for all can be understood as one continuous controversy, in the thrashing out of what is in essence the federal idea. How was a system to be devised in which the colonies/states could be part of the empire/nation—and pay their fair share in taxes for their own defense and internal improvements, while being adequately represented—but at the same time be fully self-governing in dealing with the overwhelming majority of matters which the mother country/national government had neither the ability nor the desire to administer?

Slavery, however, proved to be an Achilles' heel for the federal idea, because it went to a fundamental principle about which there had to be national uniformity—the very point Abraham Lincoln stressed in his famous "house divided" speech of 1858. In linking the defense of slavery, and later racial segregation, to the defense of state prerogatives, the South delivered a profound and lasting blow to the federal idea, and to the nation. Only in recent years, and in fits and starts, has the discourse of federalism begun to revive, partly freed of the manacles of slavery and race. It will be interesting to see if it has a future, or if the ideal of the consolidated nation-state will continue to be the principal model of political order available. For the former to happen, however, historians will have to rethink their conventional telling of the American story, which nearly always links the rise of liberty, democracy, and material prosperity exclusively with the rising power of Washington.

For additional reading, see Samuel Beer, *To Make A Nation: The Rediscovery of American Federalism* (Cambridge, Mass., 1993), a magnificent defense of the national idea, and Herbert Storing, *What the Anti-Federalists Were For* (Chicago, 1981), as well as Martin Diamond, *As Far as Republican Principles Will Admit: Essays* (Washington, D.C., 1992), which contains some of the best treatments of American federalism ever written. Significantly, however, there is no book that does for the federal idea what Herbert Croly's *The Promise of American Life* (N.Y., 1909; New Brunswick, N.J., 1999) did for the national idea.

NATURE

Nature has always been a powerful element in the way that Americans have defined themselves, especially in relation to Europe. One could, after all, redescribe early America's relatively meager past as a virtue, rather than a defect. If "nature" was opposed to "culture," then a scarcity of one meant an abundance of the other. America may not have been as sophisticated as Europe, but it *could* claim to be more "natural." Even for the New England Puritans, whose Calvinist distrust of the fallen world extended in some respects to their conception of nature, America was the New Zion in the wilderness, a place that had shaken free of the historical accretions of Anglican and Roman Catholic ecclesiology and doctrine, and therefore a place where the true and authentic apostolic Church might be restored, and the order of nature redeemed. And once the hold of Calvinist doctrine began to weaken— and there were those places where it never entirely took hold, as in Anglican Virginia—the open identification of America with "nature" became more and more pronounced. When Virginian Thomas Jefferson referred in the Declaration of Independence to "Nature and Nature's God" as the guarantors of America's "separate and equal station," and when in another context he referred to the United States as "nature's nation," he was simply stating what had become the common sense of the matter.

As the example of Jefferson suggests, the preference for "nature" dovetailed nicely with a thoroughly modern ethos based upon science, Enlightenment rationalism, and egalitarianism. What was "natural" could be opposed to what was "traditional," hieratic, and hidebound, particularly the class hierarchies of feudalism and the ecclesiastical flummeries of "revealed" religion. A "natural aristocracy," based upon natural talent rather than birth, and an easygoing "natural religion," based upon universally accessible precepts rather than privileged revelations—these, it was hoped, would characterize the emerging American genius. Lacking the European past was an advantage, not a liability.

Ralph Waldo Emerson, Henry David Thoreau, Margaret Fuller, Walt Whitman, and the other nineteenth-century prophets of American romanticism took this even further. They urged, in Emerson's words, "an original relation to the universe," expressed in "a poetry and philosophy of insight and not of tradition," an insight proceeding from knowledge of the mystic affinity or correspondence between the emotions and sentiments of the individual person and the similar dispositions in the Soul of Nature. Emerson was especially articulate in bringing out the full implications of this for the idea of America. The authentically "American Scholar," he asserted, would be a pure example of "Man Thinking," a thinker who at one and the same time exemplified romantic "self-trust" and yet spoke for the nation—an American nation in which, according to Emerson, "a nation of men will for the first time exist, because each believes himself inspired by the Divine Soul," which also animates Nature. For them too, America's closeness to Nature was her principal virtue.

In the years since, however, Nature lost some of its normative authority in American life, as romanticism waned and scientific understandings changed. Darwinian biology and Einsteinian physics have done little to support the idea of a mystic correspondence between the Soul of Nature and the souls of human beings. Indeed, in the postmodern dispensation, the very mention of "nature" is regarded in many quarters with extreme suspicion, even hostility and contempt, as nothing more than a mystification of power relations. Even so, the quasi-religious overtones of the environmental movement, and the post-1960s concern with "naturalness" in foods, clothing, and medicine—not to mention the rising interest in paganism, Native American spirituality, "deep" ecology, and the so-called Gaia hypothesis—suggest that the deification of nature has never disappeared entirely, and may even be making a comeback. In contemporary debates between those who see humans as the stewards of nature and those who see humans as the greedy and overbearing foes of nature, we may be seeing only the most recent manifestation of a long line of Christian/pagan tensions in American culture.

For additional reading, in addition to the "canonical" writings of Emerson, see Barbara Novak's marvelous *Nature and Culture: American Landscape and Painting, 1825-1875* (N.Y., 1980; revised edition, 1995), Roderick Nash, *Wilderness and the American Mind* (New Haven, Conn., 1967; third edition, 1982), Catherine Albanese's *Nature Religion in America: From the Algonkian Indians to New Age* (Chicago, 1990) and the essays in Perry Miller's *Errand into the Wilderness* (Cambridge, Mass., 1956; reprinted 1987), particularly the title essay, which

is one of the most influential short contributions to the literature of American history, and the essay "Nature and the
National Ego."

The concept of "pluralism" proposes that the national culture
of the United States ought to be able to make room for, and
leave as undisturbed as possible, robust and independent
subcultures, usually those based on race, ethnicity, religion,
or country of origin—and often all four at once. A commitment to a high degree of cultural pluralism is now thought to
be one of America's defining characteristics. But such an
assertion would have taken the Founders by surprise. They
did not set out to make America a great colossus of cultural
pluralism. Instead, it happened almost entirely without
anyone intending it to. It happened mainly because an
enormous, resource-rich, and thinly populated continent
was eager to procure immigrant labor from anyplace it could
get it, including settlers from non-English-speaking and
non-Protestant countries, and even African laborers who were
enslaved or indentured. Such beginnings virtually ensured
that issues of race, ethnicity, and pluralism would hold a
central and persistent place in American history.

It is no coincidence that the cultural tensions represented
by the interplay of those three terms echo the political tensions flowing from the attempt to form a "composition" of
nation and federation (see above). By the time the United
States became a nation, it had already acquired many forms of

internal diversity that it could not possibly have disavowed, even if it had wanted to. And so it was not for nothing that the new nation adopted the motto *E Pluribus Unum*: out of many, one. Just as a workable U.S. Constitution somehow had to accommodate itself to the preexisting reality of independent states, so a workable American society somehow had to accommodate racial and ethnic diversity that was already in place. To be sure, the nation at the time of the Founding was overwhelmingly British in character, a fact of enormous consequence for the institutional and cultural shape of the new nation. But so long as it had an abundance of land, a scarcity of labor, and an appetite for economic growth, the new nation was likely to find its racial and ethnic makeup becoming progressively more and more complex. And it did. Thanks to numerous waves of immigration in the more than two centuries since the Revolution, along with the restless geographical and social mobility so characteristic of Americans, personal identity in America has come to be a remarkably multifaceted thing. To be an American generally means operating on several different planes at once. A Virginian can be an American, and also a Southerner, and also a Polish Catholic, and possibly a Mason too. And he may take a residual loyalty to these things with him, when he moves to Pennsylvania, and later retires to Florida. Far from being unusual, such combinations are the commonest things imaginable.

Pluralism, then, was a social reality long before it became a normative ideal. Indeed, until fairly recently, the way Americans thought about their nation's ever-growing ethnic and racial diversity—to the extent that they regarded it as a positive thing at all, rather than a contamination of Anglo-Saxon purity—was more likely to resemble the ideal of "the melting pot," which assimilated all cultural differences into a single rich alloy. The image was immortalized in Israel Zangwill's 1908 play of the same name, but the general concept is much older. As early as the 1780s, one finds in the writings of J. Hector St. John de Crèvecoeur an affirmation of the American as a "new man," whose sturdy character was a blend of all the nation's various cultural elements. Such a concept, which made a virtue of necessity, was a thumb in the eye of racial purists who deplored the "mongrel" quality of American culture. It was also, at least theoretically, a challenge to the ideal of Anglo-Saxon dominance, since everyone, even the scions of old New England families, was subject to a meltdown-and-mingling with all other elements, thereby to be transformed into something new.

So went the theory. But the melting-pot cultural ideal had three problems. First, it did not accurately describe what was actually taking place. Immigrants simply were *not* abandoning all of their native characteristics when they came to America. They did *not* blend without a trace into the great American family, at least not in a mere generation or two. Instead, many of them continued to live, work, eat, play, and worship as people apart, "unmelted," dwelling in their own ethnic enclaves. Second, even as a theory, the melting-pot ideal seemed to stop short at the boundaries of racial difference. For all its seeming inclusiveness, the ideal generally ex-

cluded African Americans and others whose racial characteristics were deemed to be too far outside the Anglo-Saxon mold.
The interest in colonization schemes shown by Abraham Lincoln and other reformers, plans which would have removed
African Americans from the continent entirely, shows how
ingrained were these prejudices based upon race, and how
limited was the range of human types the ideal was actually
willing to entertain. And third, the assimilation actually being demanded of immigrants was more of an indoctrination
into mainstream Anglo-Protestant culture than even the most
compassionate observers ever wanted to acknowledge. The rise
of Catholic parochial education, for example, came in response
to a perception that the public schools were, even with a
practice as seemingly innocuous as Bible-reading, inculcating
a kind of soft-core cultural Protestantism that was damaging
to the long-term prospects of American Catholicism.

Not long after the turn of the twentieth century, all of
these misgivings linked up with the revolt of intellectuals
against the constraints of a primarily Anglo-Saxon "genteel
tradition," and the result was the rise of anti-assimilationist
doctrines of cultural pluralism or "transnationality." As early
as 1915 the German-Jewish immigrant Horace Kallen, the chief
proponent of cultural pluralism, was comparing American
culture to a vast and various symphony orchestra, whose musical
richness was enhanced precisely by the tonal distinctiveness of
each of its members. The melting pot, he felt, even if it worked
as claimed, would destroy that symphonic richness, and substitute for it a bland and homogeneous unison. There was of

course the need for some kind of national culture, just as there was a need for a national government. But Kallen and other pluralists assumed that such a national culture could be thin and limited in character, allowing the richness and depth of more particular affiliations to be preserved.

Kallen's was a decidedly minority view during the 1920s, an era far better known for its nativism and its immigration-restriction statutes. It remained largely submerged until the 1960s, when a powerful interest in racial and ethnic identity resurfaced on the national agenda, far outrunning the civil-rights movement that had stimulated it. By the 1980s those doctrines had found popular form in the idea of "multiculturalism," an ill-defined and slippery word which could mean almost anything one wanted it to mean, from taking a generous view of ethnic foods and customs to believing in the absolute cognitive separateness of the "cultures" making up modern American society. In its milder forms, multiculturalism seems fairly unexceptionable, although one cannot help but notice, even there, that the shift away from the 1960s language of "integration" toward the language of "multiculturalism" reflects a different, and more diffuse, ideal of inclusion. In its more strident forms, such as the movement to teach a self-consciously mythological "Afrocentric" history in the public schools, or more generally, the claim that the discourses of various oppressed groups are off-limits to the critiques of outsiders, multiculturalism is deeply subversive of public life, and of the very possibility of a pluralistic American nationhood—not to mention the idea of history as truth, and not merely group therapy.

It seems unlikely that such an extreme position can prevail for long, particularly outside the strange hothouse of academia, where even the most implausible plants can flourish for a time. But like many such exaggerations, multiculturalism serves to raise a very useful question: How much of a uniform national culture does American society really *need?* Given that neither an extreme multiculturalism nor an extreme assimilationism is acceptable, then where, in the continuum between the two, should one locate the optimal point of balance? How does one protect, at one and the same time, both the *distinctiveness* of racial and ethnic groups and their full *membership*, both collectively and individually, in the national polity? How much homogeneity is necessary to produce solid citizens and preserve a workable social harmony? How much distinctiveness is compatible with both social order and social equity? Is it still important, for example, to use the schools and other agencies of public education to form a robust, clearly defined civic identity in the minds of all Americans, including a "canon" of essential knowledge? Or is it better to insist only on a clear but minimal standard of citizenship, and then leave the rest to civil society and private life?

It is striking to realize, once again, how closely such questions parallel the very issues raised by the tension between the national and federative ideas in American politics. All of which simply goes to show that, in America, multiple loyalties are not only commonplace, but are the *spécialité de la maison*. When W. E. B. Du Bois wrote hauntingly in *The*

Souls of Black Folk about his experience of "doubleness" as a black American, he told a tale whose particulars were very much his own. But its algebra has proven surprisingly universal.

For additional reading, in addition to the "canonical" works of Du Bois and Ralph Ellison, see Richard Rodriguez's poignant memoir, *The Hunger of Memory: The Education of Richard Rodriguez* (Boston, 1981; N.Y., 1988), David Hollinger's *Postethnic America: Beyond Multiculturalism* (N.Y., 1995), Thomas Sowell's brilliant (and shamefully neglected) *Race and Culture: A World View* (University Park, Pa., 1992; N.Y., 1994), and Leon Wieseltier's *Against Identity* (N.Y., 1996).

REDEEMER NATION

The notion that America is a nation chosen by God, a New Israel destined for a providential mission of world redemption, has been a near-constant element in American history. The persistence of such a notion is a clear indication of the nation's deep roots in Protestant theology and practices. The Reformation, in stressing the authority of the Scriptures, drew renewed attention to the biblical idea of the millennium, the thousand-year earthly reign of Christ that was to come at the conclusion of human history, as foretold in the Book of Revelation. Those biblical passages are, of course, notoriously difficult to interpret. But their practical effects were less ambiguous. Belief in a coming earthly millennium, however one understood the details of it, transformed one's conception of earthly history, filling it with an electric sense of expectancy that God was going to redeem *this* world, and that His redeeming work could begin at any moment—and indeed, might already be fully underway. Such feelings of expectancy were common among the Protestants who settled in the British North American colonies, especially those in New England, who saw their "errand into the wilderness" as an instrument in God's plan to cleanse and redeem the Old World's corruption of His church.

It was only natural that, in time, the inhabitants of Massachusetts Bay's "city upon a hill" would expand their sense of historical accountability and come to see themselves, and their nation, as collective bearers of a world-historical destiny. What is more surprising, however, is how persistent that self-understanding would prove to be. The same convictions can be found in the rhetoric of the American Revolution, in the vision of Manifest Destiny, in the crusading sentiments of Civil War intellectuals, in the benevolent imperialism of *fin de siècle* apostles of Christian civilization, and in the fervent speeches of President Woodrow Wilson at the time of the First World War. No one expressed the idea more directly, however, than Senator Albert J. Beveridge of Indiana, who told the United States Senate, in the wake of the Spanish-American War, that God "has marked the American people as His chosen nation to finally lead in the redemption of the world."

Most astonishing of all is the fact that this crusading impulse has survived largely intact, even into an age in which its original religious basis is almost completely gone—indeed, in which the missionary past of Protestant Christianity is regarded with horror by crusading secularists. Few presidents since Wilson's day have cared to make a direct appeal to Americans' sense of chosenness by God as a justification for American action in the world. But their sense of America's larger moral responsibility, particularly its open-ended obligation to uphold human rights, defend democracy, and impart American-style institutions, technologies, and values to the rest of the world, seems undiminished. To be sure, there are other strains of thought about these matters, including a sober "realist" tradition grounded in John Quincy Adams's famous assertion that America "does not go abroad in search of monsters to destroy." For better or worse, however—and there are elements of both—the "redeemer nation" paradigm has been the more resilient.

Perhaps part of its resiliency stems from the fact that the providential understanding of America points simultaneously in two different directions. Should America resolve to be a nation apart, a Fortress America whose moral superiority is secured by its distance from decadent Europe and the world? Or should America devote its political, economic, cultural, military, and spiritual superiority precisely to the moral transformation of the world? To put it in a deliberately extreme and tendentious form: Should America attempt to keep its soul pure by keeping the world at arm's length? Or should it keep its soul pure by purifying the world, and making that world (in Woodrow Wilson's words) fit to live in?

This way of putting matters is admittedly grossly unfair, if for no other reason than that it seems to discount the enormous good that the United States has done, and will continue to do, in the world. But putting it this way has one great advantage: it demonstrates how much the two great supposed diplomatic opposites—isolationism and interventionism— have in common with one another, and how little either has in common with a "realistic" foreign policy that hard-headedly calculates national policy on the basis of national interests. As was observed already, nearly all Americans, whether they are on the Left or the Right, have a hard time thinking of their country as "just another nation." The persistence of this way of thinking about America has always been, and will continue to be, an enormous factor to contend with in the formulation and execution of our foreign policy.

For additional reading, in addition to the previously mentioned works of Perry Miller, see Ernest Lee Tuveson, *Redeemer Nation: The Idea of America's Millenial Role* (Chicago, 1968; reprinted 1980), Conrad Cherry, *God's New Israel: Religious Interpretations of American Destiny* (Englewood Cliffs, N.J., 1971; revised edition, 1998), and a superb synthesis, Walter A. McDougall's *Promised Land, Crusader State: The American Encounter with the World Since 1776* (Boston, 1997).

RELIGION

In light of the preceding entry, it would seem wildly implausible to report that American historical scholarship over the years has largely neglected the study of religion. Yet it is sadly true. Aside from a handful of moments in American history, notably the founding of New England, where mention of the religious dimension is unavoidable, precious little in the story of American history that survives in our standard textbooks even hints at the strong and abiding religiosity of the American people. It is not clear whether this fact reflects a commitment to philosophical secularism, or merely to methodological secularism, among the overwhelming majority of academic historians. But it does indicate an enormous gap between such historians and the rest of the American people, given that public-opinion polls indicate with numbing regularity that an overwhelming majority of Americans, usually in excess of 90 percent, claim to believe in a personal God and in the veracity of the Bible.

Historians are, of course, not required to consult the *vox populi*. But it would seem that in this case they have missed the mark badly. So prevalent, for example, was the standard understanding of the Founding as a strictly secular event, in which a band of American *philosophes* installed a deliberately godless Constitution, that it came as a shocking revelation to many scholars when the Library of Congress mounted its magnificent 1998 exhibit, "Religion and the Founding of the American Republic," which convincingly demonstrated in stunning detail, through a profusion of artwork and texts, just how deeply religious our forebears had been. This very event seems to have represented a turning of the tide, though one that has perhaps been long in preparation. It is not a coincidence, after all, that so many of our finest American historians today are historians of religion—George Marsden, Mark Noll, Nathan Hatch, Harry Stout, D. G. Hart, Patrick Allitt, Nancy Ammerman, R. Laurence Moore, Joel Carpenter, and numerous others. Their labors are now bearing fruit.

It needs to be added, of course, that an interest in religion, and a commitment to acknowledging its importance as an object of study, does not necessarily entail religious *belief* (though it should not preclude belief either). Perry Miller, whose passionate scholarship rescued the study of Puritanism from its descent into banal superficiality, was a committed secularist and atheist. And yet, the scope of the Library of Congress exhibition suggests that there may well be more at stake than merely bringing fairness and balance to a neglected subject. Instead, American historians need to acknowledge the *central importance* of religious commitments to Americans, past and present, and to do so without reductionism or condescension.

To do so is to recover a rather old insight. Tocqueville in fact asserted that religion was the first and most important of democratic institutions. Europeans in his day were abandoning religious faith and practice, in the mistaken belief that the "spirit of liberty" was incompatible with the authoritarian "spirit of religion." Tocqueville's visit to America convinced him that the opposite was true. In America, religious beliefs and institutions restrained individual self-assertion in ways that made the exercise of freedom more stable and more effective. In a society that had clearly separated church and state, the "spirit of liberty" and the "spirit of religion" would actually reinforce one another. Liberty supported religion by making it voluntary, the democratic form of assent. But religion was also needed to support liberty, both as a source of independent support for the free will, and because the "moral tie" binding a society had to be strengthened precisely "in proportion as the political tie is relaxed."

Such were the benefits of nonestablishment to the growth of religious faith in America, as opposed to, say, France. The voluntarism of American religion has made it flourish. But the same voluntarism, as a legacy of the country's primarily dissenting Protestant origins, has also made American religion incredibly fractious, division-prone, and consumer-oriented. The story of American Protestantism in particular is a vexing story of one church quarrel after another, nearly always eventuating in bitter division, mitosis without end. Which suggests why the larger story line of American religious history is the collapse of Protestant dominance, which has gradually yielded ground first to Roman Catholicism (now the largest Christian denomination in the United States), then to a vague Judeo-Christian tradition, and then to more and more wide-open religious pluralism, which has moved far beyond Judeo-Christian limits. R. Laurence Moore has even gone so far as to argue that it is the "outsiders" who best represent what is distinctive about American religion.

There is truth in that. But the emerging new/old view of the American Founding suggests that the ultimate *insiders* were also deeply religious men, whose biblical faith played an integral role in their thinking, and therefore in the institutions they went on to shape. So too were the Americans who drove the movement to abolish slavery and to abolish racial segregation. Much of the country's moral heritage derives from that same source. Too much for historians, or anyone else, to ignore.

For additional reading, see Nathan O. Hatch, *The Democratization of American Christianity* (New Haven, Conn., 1989); R. Laurence Moore, *Religious Outsiders and the Making of Americans* (N.Y., 1986), George M. Marsden, *Fundamentalism and American Culture: The Shaping of Twentieth-Century Evangelicalism, 1870-1925* (N.Y., 1980), Henry Feingold, *Zion in America: The Jewish Experience from Colonial Times to the Present* (N.Y., 1974; revised edition, 1981), Robert Wuthnow, *The Restructuring of American Religion: Society and Faith Since World War II* (Princeton, N.J., 1988), and James H. Hutson and Sara Day, *Religion and the Founding of the American Republic* (Washington, D.C., 1998), which has a foreword by Jaroslav Pelikan.

REVOLUTION

The fact that the United States gained its independence through the first of the great revolutions against a European colonial power is both a source of pride and confusion to Americans. Pride because it was a brave, assertive, risk-taking act, which at the same time would seem to place us in the forefront of the world struggle for democracy and human liberation. And yet there is confusion, because the United States has not played the role of, shall we say, Cuba in the modern world—nor have Americans wanted it to. There is a certain implicit, if inchoate, understanding that the American Revolution was not *that* kind of revolution, and that

America does not promote *that* kind of revolution.

So if it was not *that* kind of revolution, then what kind *was* it? Or was there even a "revolution" at all? On this interesting point, historians disagree sharply, and there will be no substitute for your learning something about the vast and immensely rich historiography of the past century or so, to get a handle on the issue. The key questions, though, are easily stated. Is the American Revolution best understood as an event within the British Empire, which was caused by errors or problems or inevitable flaws in the imperial structure of governance? Was the main point to restore the fundamental rights of Englishmen, which were being threatened both in the colonies and at home? Or is it an event better understood on strictly American grounds, as a more or less full-fledged, class-conflict-driven, *social* revolution and contest for power? Was it, to adapt a familiar slogan, fundamentally a question of American home rule—or of which Americans would rule at home? And just how much fundamental political, social, and cultural change really resulted from it?

The way one regards the Declaration of Independence is a good point of entrance into these issues too. Does the disparity between the Declaration's ringing endorsement of natural rights and the Constitution's silent acceptance of slavery indicate that the latter document, and the people pushing it, were betraying, or backing away from, the revolutionary fervor of the former? Or do we thereby read far too much significance into the Declaration, a document that does not seem to have been regarded as authoritative in its own time, out of desire to find a contemporary precedent for our own egalitarianism? Whatever the answers, the meaning of the Revolution—and the meaning of "revolution" for Americans—will likely continue to be both a touchstone and a point of contention.

For additional reading, to give one a sampling of the range of possibilities, see Daniel Boorstin, *The Genius of American Politics* (Chicago, 1953; reprinted 1967), Bernard Bailyn, *The Ideological Origins of the American Revolution* (Cambridge, Mass., 1967; enlarged edition, 1992), Gordon Wood, *The Radicalism of the American Revolution* (N.Y., 1992, reprinted 1993), and Pauline Maier, *American Scripture: Making the Declaration of Independence* (N.Y., 1997).

SELF-MAKING

In the modern era, the self is increasingly regarded as the sole source of moral value. This is a problem, for more than one reason. Not only does it reduce moral reasoning to a matter of subjective taste and emotion, but it places an impossible burden on an inherently unstable concept. Indeed, one of the most powerful themes of postmodernism is its assertion that the modern self cannot bear the weight placed upon it by fragmented modern life, and that in fact, the multiplicity of our world *requires* us to operate on the basis of multiple selves. René Descartes inaugurated modernity with the assertion that the "I" is the most fundamental building block in our apprehension of reality, the still point in a moving world. Now it appears that the self, far from being foundational, is the most protean and variable thing of all. In the postmodern view, the search for "individual integrity" and "authenticity" is outmoded. The postmodern self is not a unitary thing, but an ever-shifting ensemble of social roles—a disorderly venue in which the healthy ego functions less as a commander in chief than as a skilled air-traffic controller.

It is hard to imagine how previous generations of Americans, from colonial times to the mid-twentieth century, would have responded to such statements. In all likelihood, they would have found them ludicrous—or horrifying. For the idea of self-making—not only as in the much-maligned idea of the "self-made man," but the related ideas of "self-improvement" and "self-culture"—is absolutely central to American thought and culture. One can begin with two of the archetypal figures of colonial American cultural history—Jonathan Edwards and Benjamin Franklin—and find in the writings of both a powerful concern with the process of conscious self-molding, which involved a subduing and controlling of the negative features of their natures. One sees the same concerns with "self-culture," elaborated or expanded, in most of the great writers and political figures of the nineteenth century, from William Ellery Channing, the evangelical Whigs, and Abraham Lincoln, to Horace Bushnell and James Freeman Clarke. One sees the impulse toward self-improvement not only in the famous charts and tables of Franklin (which Thoreau mocked, without himself deviating one jot from the gospel of self-making), but in the letters and diaries of countless lesser-known Americans. Self-making, then, which includes in its portfolio the possibility of rising in the world precisely as far as one's abilities and pluck will take one, is a quintessentially American value, one that resonates through just about every other element of American history—liberty, equality, immigration, social class, attitudes toward Europe, and so on.

It does, however, have its dark side. Franklin himself understood that in a fluid world where one's family and antecedents are no longer a relevant datum, it might become more important to have the *appearance* of virtue, a form of self-presentation that one could manipulate, than to have the virtue itself. Hence, there is a temptation to yield to superficiality and fakery; the "confidence man" was a nineteenth-century type who specialized in betraying the very confidence that he won. In the end, such an individual might sell his very soul in order to buy a more useful self. No book has captured that aspect of the American experience, the self-mortification, self-denial, and self-hatred that are involved in the act of radical self-making, than F. Scott Fitzgerald's "canonical" novel, *The Great Gatsby*, one of the truly indispensable books about America.

In a sense, *Gatsby* was part of an American countertradition, running against our "official" optimism, reasserting the intransigence of history, the intractability of reality, and the inescapable price of things. Fitzgerald, who was in many ways a Victorian (and Puritan) at heart, understood that self-making had its limits, even if he showed little inclination to observe such limits in his own self-destructive life. But he was wise enough to fear that when the act of self-making is cut loose entirely from the improvement of a person who is *real*, and when it is permitted to treat the soul as something entirely plastic, it becomes something monstrous and inhuman. In one stroke, it transforms the greatest source of human dignity—our capacity for self-overcoming and self-transformation—into its greatest enemy.

The colonial, Revolutionary, and Victorian American writers who extolled self-making did so with an understanding of the soul as having a certain inherent structure, with its own hardness and inflexibility, and its own enduring propensities for evil and sloth. The building of character was a slow process, the patient boring of boards; and it operated within a moral universe that was fairly universal and fairly unambiguous. There were moral and practical limits to what it could properly accomplish. But what if now there are no limits? What if there is no coherent idea of the self anymore, and no binding transpersonal moral code, so that what goes by the name of self-making and self-control is henceforth to be turned over to the pharmacologists and genetic engineers? Then those concepts become instruments in what C. S. Lewis called "the abolition of man." Self-making will have been a victim of its own success.

For additional reading, see Daniel Walker Howe, *Making the American Self: Jonathan Edwards to Abraham Lincoln* (Cambridge, Mass., 1997), Kenneth S. Lynn, *The Dream of Success: A Study of the Modern American Imagination* (Boston, 1955; Westport, Conn., 1972), Barry Alan Shain, *The Myth of American Individualism: The Protestant Origins of American Political Thought* (Princeton, N.J., 1994), Christopher Lasch, *The Cul-*

ture of Narcissism: American Life in an Age of Diminishing Expectations (N.Y., 1978; reprinted with a new afterword, 1991), Sherry Turkle, *Life on the Screen: Identity in the Age of the Internet* (N.Y., 1995, reprinted 1997), Wilfred M. McClay, *The Masterless: Self and Society in Modern America* (Chapel Hill, N.C., 1994), and Charles Taylor, *Sources of the Self: The Making of the Modern Identity* (Cambridge, Mass., 1989; reprinted 1992).

THE SOUTH

One could legitimately have included a "window" in this collection dealing with sectionalism or regionalism in American history, and one for each of the nation's distinctive regions: New England, the Midwest, the Great Plains, the West, and so on. But in the end, there is one region that, more than any other, has endured, maintained its cultural identity, and contributed to the cultural treasury of the nation—and that is the South. Geographically, the South is not easy to define with precision. It is not exactly the same as the old Confederacy, since non-Confederate border states such as Missouri, Kentucky, and Maryland, as well as the Indian Territory that eventually became the state of Oklahoma, came to have enduringly Southern characteristics, as do even the southernmost parts of Illinois and Indiana. There are significant differences among Southern states—one thinks of, say, Texas and Virginia—to which one must add that, in Southern states such as Louisiana and Florida, one has to go north to go south, culturally speaking, since the southernmost parts of those states are not really Southern.

Nor is it easy to say exactly when the South became "the South" in Americans' minds. But certainly by the time the Constitution had been adopted, and the Northern states had abolished slavery, the two sections had begun to diverge. This was almost immediately reflected not only in growing inter-sectional antagonism over economic issues, but also in issues of regional identity. While Northerners deplored the South's use of slave labor as an anachronism and moral evil, Southern-ers (or at any rate, Southern intellectuals) increasingly mounted a defense that presented the South as a defender of pre-mod-ern, organic, hierarchical institutions, in contrast to the North's inhuman and exploitative free-labor, cash-nexus economy.

There was myth and exaggeration in such defenses, but even so, they accurately reflected the growth of a very distinc-tive civilization in the Old South: one that was less urban, more agricultural, economically underdeveloped, strikingly biracial, and strongly hierarchical, with a clear-cut ladder of social organization, marked disparities of wealth and poverty, and a powerful guiding ethos (in the white elites) that melded the ubiquitous Protestant Christianity with neomedieval chivalric ideals, including especially a fierce and combative sense of honor. From the time that the South emerged as a distinct region with distinctive folkways, it played an impor-tant role in the national identity, by serving as the opposite number or "the Other," against which modern American egali-tarian and free-labor ideals could define themselves.

Its cultural distinctiveness survived the Civil War, and survived well into the twentieth century. The generosity of

Southern entertaining, the gregarious warmth of Southern social relations, the respectful formality of Southern manners, the vitality of Southern family life, the emotive and evangelical quality of Southern religion—these differentia are not myths, and they are to a striking degree characteristics shared by nearly all Southerners, black and white. Nor, alas, is the relative poverty and marginalization of African Americans a point of differentiation between North and South. If anything, there is reason to believe that racial healing may have brighter prospects in the South than in the Northern cities, a statement that would have seemed absurd in the 1950s.

But all of that said, it is not clear how long the South's distinctiveness will persist in the twenty-first century. The city of Atlanta was once a potent symbol of Southern victimization at the hands of the marauding General William T. Sherman. Now it is an icon of Sunbelt business prosperity, a by-word for marauding sprawl and frenetic growth, and an emblem of the globalization of news propagation and consciousness-molding, in the form of the all-pervasive Atlanta-based Cable News Network—an organization that is about as Southern as a reindeer herd. Such a transformation does not bode well for Southern distinctiveness.

So some kind of cultural assimilation to the American (and global-American) ethos is underway. And yet, given the strong ascendency of certain elements of Southern culture—one need only think, for example, of the extraordinary power of the South in national politics, or of the domination of American (and world) popular music in recent years by Southern-derived forms such as blues, rock-n-roll, country-western, bluegrass, etc.—it is not always clear whether the South is Americanizing, or America is Southernizing. Perhaps a bit of both.

For additional reading, see William R. Taylor's *Cavalier and Yankee: The Old South and American National Character* (N.Y., 1961; revised edition, 1993), Edward L. Ayers's *Southern Crossing: A History of the American South, 1877-1906* (Oxford, 1995), Eugene D. Genovese's *The Southern Tradition: The Achievement and Limitations of an American Conservatism* (Cambridge, Mass., 1994), John Shelton Reed's *The Enduring South: Subcultural Persistence in Mass Society* (Lexington, Mass., 1972; Chapel Hill, N.C., 1986), Kenneth S. Lynn's *Mark Twain and Southwestern Humor* (Boston, 1959; Westport, Conn., 1972), David M. Potter's *The South and the Sectional Conflict* (Baton Rouge, La., 1968), C. Vann Woodward's *The Burden of Southern History* (Baton Rouge, La., 1960; reprinted 1993), W. J. Cash's *The Mind of the South* (N.Y., 1941; reprinted 1991), Tony Horowitz's *Confederates in the Attic: Dispatches from the Unfinished Civil War* (N.Y., 1999), and the irresistible *Encyclopedia of Southern Culture* (Chapel Hill, N.C., 1989; N.Y., 1991), edited by Charles Reagan Wilson.

CAVEATS

HEREIN I OFFER a few useful observations about the practical aspects of historical study, presented in negative form. I choose to emphasize caveats, rather than dos and don'ts, because falsehood is easier to identify than truth; and it is easier to specify how one *shouldn't* do history than to say how one *should*.

Caveat 1: Avoid using the term "political correctness" to describe an argument or position that seems to you contrived or ideologically motivated. First, because it is a kind of *argumentum ad hominem*, which fails to engage the issue at hand on rational terms, preferring instead to cast doubt on the motives of the one who offers it. This kind of argument can rebound upon those who use it, and eventually render discussion impossible. Second, because the use of such a term relies upon the lamentable assumption that all orthodoxies are *ipso facto* coercive and illegitimate. And that is false. It is a particularly strange development when campus conservatives, who are generally thought to look with sympathy upon orthodoxy, end up branding their opponents' views as attempts to impose an orthodoxy. This is a lazy and uncivil way of arguing, even when it is accurate (as, alas, it usually is). The emphasis should not be on the inherent wrongness of *any* orthodoxy *per se*, but the wrong of the *particular* ideas that a particular orthodoxy is advocating. These days, defending the possibility of a reasoned orthodoxy may be the most radical position of all.

Caveat 2: Ignore the near-universal assumption that, when it comes to scholarship, newest is best. This is one of the many distortions wrought upon our intellectual life, both inside and outside the academy, by our obsession with fashion and "originality." It also reflects the suffocating arrogance and self-absorption of the present, an arrogance and self-absorption that afflicts professional historians as much as anyone else. It is an especially potent trap for graduate students, who are anxiously trying to figure out where, and if, they fit in "the profession," and who therefore tend to be overly attentive to the cues of their advisors. For an antidote, read Jaroslav Pelikan's marvelous book *The Vindication of Tradition* (New Haven, Conn., 1984), the fruit of a lifetime's reflection by a scholar's scholar, which strikes a sensible balance between a hidebound traditionalism and a feckless chasing after what is merely new.

Caveat 3: Beware of historiographical essays, which are useful in placing a series of books in a larger context of scholarly debate, but all too often do so at the expense of providing a careful and nuanced account of the books in question. Much of the drama and back-and-forth of such essays is entirely ginned-up by the author, who typically takes one element of a historian's argument out of context, exaggerates it, then deploys an equally out-of-context exaggeration of another historian's book, as a counter-argument—and then, the next thing you know, there are neatly quarrelling "schools," fighting it out over rival simplistic assertions. The resulting effect is that of a Punch and Judy show, in which the puppets are all talking books, whose flapping covers fling out words that have been placed there by others. Graduate training typically devotes too much of its time to teaching students how to repeat and construct these rather fanciful narratives, which too often serve as a substitute for careful reading of carefully written books, particularly older books that the graduate instructor regards as unworthy of sustained attention. (See Caveat 2.) Just grin and bear such things, and don't take them very seriously. Keep in mind that today's "pathbreaking" books will receive the same dismissive treatment in another five years.

Caveat 4: Place as little stock as you possibly can in the bureaucratization of historical inquiry, which has divided history into such subfields as diplomatic history, military history, political history, economic history, social history, cultural history, intellectual history, women's history, and so on. To be sure, these and other such labels are indispensable descriptive categories, and given the volume of scholarship being published, if you are an aspiring scholar, you will have to take your stand within one of them (and within a nationality and time period as well). It is entirely possible that a good, even great, historian will spend all of his or her career writing entirely within one of these categories. My only point is to remember at all times the distinction between the many ways we slice and dice historical study, and the multidimensional character of the past itself. You have an obligation to learn as much as you can about *all* these dimensions.

Caveat 5: If your teachers insist that to be a good historian, you have to approach a subject without any preconceptions, take it with a grain of salt. They mean well, but I've found that this is not helpful advice. Not only is it not practical to approach a subject without preconceptions, it is not desirable, particularly if you are writing a research paper or thesis. Without hunches and other preconceptions, you have no way of organizing your inquiry, no way of filtering or selecting out from the flow of information, no idea of what to look for in your prospective subject, no way of zeroing in on insightful hypotheses. The success of any inquiry, historical or otherwise, depends upon the richness of the questions it asks, and the hypotheses it proposes, because it is the questions and hypotheses that structure the inquiry, by giving the evidence something to say "yes" or "no" to. Hence, the key to being a good historian is most emphatically *not* to approach a subject without preconceptions. The key, rather, is to follow your hunches, let them lead you forward into your research—but at the same time, rigorously withhold *judgment*, always being open to bad news, to disconfirmation, to the possibility that your preconceptions are not being fulfilled. And when the bad news comes in, as it reliably does, be willing to surrender your hunches without too traumatic a fight, and adapt your hypotheses to what your research is showing you. What starts out as bold self-indulgence turns into endless asceticism. You have to learn to entertain both qualities of mind at once. Together, little by little, they will lead you in the direction of the truth.

Caveat 6: None of the above should be taken to imply that you should blithely ignore the counsel and direction of your teachers. Not only is this imprudent, for obvious reasons, but it is wrong. Even the most egregious teachers have something to teach you, and you will learn nothing from them through acts of mindless rebellion. Make allowances for the frailty of human nature. (You will need such allowances yourself, later on in life.) In any event, you will have your chance to speak your own mind in due course. Be prepared to make the most of it.

AN AMERICAN CANON

NOTHING STIRS THE scholarly juices more than discussions of what does or does not belong in a "canon." Etymologically, the word refers to a measuring stick or standard, but the current usage is meant to echo the "canon of Holy Scripture," those books of the Bible judged by the Church to be divinely inspired and therefore doctrinally authoritative. That derivation explains why the term "canon" is almost never used unironically in today's academy, where the very idea of *any* orthodoxy or other authority is deemed a *prima facie* affront. (See Caveat 1.) In some circles, the very idea of a canon is viewed as inherently coercive, and those advocating one are thought to have all but donned the brown shirt. Be that as it may, I've found that students, who generally can tell when a seeming liberality is really just a mask for indifference, appreciate such lists. So let me be clear: I make no claim for the following works as either divinely inspired or doctrinally authoritative. But every one of them seems to me a book that a serious student of American history and society ought to have read, marked, learned, and inwardly digested.

In addition, it may not be entirely fanciful to observe

that the word "canon" has other meanings. One of them is musical. A canon is a melody devised, like a round, in such a way that when it is repeated by different voices, with each of those repetitions staggered so that they overlap in time, the result is an elaborate and unexpected counterpoint—produced entirely out of itself. In that sense, these books too comprise a canon of sorts, whose repetition and elaboration will yet yield fresh insights, and new harmonies and dissonances, along with the old ones.

Henry Adams, *The Education of Henry Adams*
James Bryce, *The American Commonwealth*
Whittaker Chambers, *Witness*
John Dewey, *The Child and the Curriculum* and
    The School and Society
Frederick Douglass, *Narrative*
W. E. B. Du Bois, *The Souls of Black Folk*
Ralph Ellison, *Invisible Man*
Ralph Waldo Emerson, *Nature* and *Essays, First Series*
F. Scott Fitzgerald, *The Great Gatsby*
Benjamin Franklin, *The Autobiography*
Alexander Hamilton, James Madison, and John Jay,
    The Federalist
Nathaniel Hawthorne, *The Scarlet Letter*
William James, *Pragmatism*
D. H. Lawrence, *Studies in Classic American Literature*
Abraham Lincoln, *Speeches and Writings*
Herman Melville, *Moby-Dick*

Perry Miller and Thomas Johnson, eds., *The Puritans*

David Riesman, et al., *The Lonely Crowd*

George Santayana, "The Genteel Tradition in American
  Philosophy" and *Character and Opinion in the
  United States*

Harriet Beecher Stowe, *Uncle Tom's Cabin*

Henry David Thoreau, *Walden*

Alexis de Tocqueville, *Democracy in America*

Mark Twain, *The Adventures of Huckleberry Finn*

Booker T. Washington, *Up from Slavery*

Walt Whitman, *Leaves of Grass* and *Democratic Vistas*

Richard Wright, *Black Boy*

In addition, I recommend that you acquire a copy of the two volumes of David Hollinger and Charles Capper, eds., *The American Intellectual Tradition* (N.Y., 1989; third edition, 1997), which is a conveniently organized, judiciously selected, and usefully annotated collection of some of the most influential American works and writers, put together by two of our best intellectual historians.

EMBARKING ON A LIFELONG PURSUIT OF KNOWLEDGE?

Take Advantage of These New Resources & a New Website

❧

The ISI Guides to the Major Disciplines are part of the Intercollegiate Studies Institute's (ISI) **Student Self-Reliance Project**, an integrated, sequential program of educational supplements designed to guide students in making key decisions that will enable them to acquire an appreciation of the accomplishments of Western civilization.

Developed with fifteen months of detailed advice from college professors and students, these resources provide advice in course selection and guidance in actual coursework. The Project elements can be used independently by students to navigate the existing university curriculum in a way that deepens their understanding of our Western intellectual heritage. As indicated below, the Project's integrated components will answer key questions at each stage of a student's education.

What are the strengths and weaknesses of the most selective schools?
Choosing the Right College directs prospective college students to the best and worst that top American colleges have to offer.

What is the essence of a liberal arts education?
A Student's Guide to Liberal Learning introduces students to the vital connection between liberal education and political liberty.

What core courses should every student take?
A Student's Guide to the Core Curriculum instructs students how to build their own core curriculum, utilizing electives available at virtually every university, and how to identify and overcome contemporary political biases in those courses.

How can students learn from the best minds in their major field of study?
Study Guides to the Major Disciplines introduces students to overlooked and misrepresented classics, facilitating work within their majors. Guides currently in production assess the fields of literature, political philosophy, European and American history, and economics.

Which great modern thinkers are neglected?
The Library of Modern Thinkers introduces students to great minds who have contributed to the literature of the West and who are neglected or denigrated in today's classroom. Figures included in this series are Robert Nisbet, Eric Voegelin, Wilhelm Roepke, Ludwig von Mises, Will Herberg, and many others.

In order to address the academic problems faced by every student in an ongoing manner, a new website, **www.collegeguide.org**, has been launched. It offers easy access to unparalleled resources for making the most of one's college experience—and it features an interactive component that will allow students to pose questions about academic life on America's college campuses.

These features make ISI a one-stop organization for serious students of all ages. Visit **www.isi.org** or call **1-800-526-7022** and add your name to the 50,000-plus ISI network of teachers, students, and professors.